Window Shopping for God is a mesmer
ing honesty, poignancy and yes, the trademark Kimmett hilarity.
Addiction, birth, death, Catholics, Buddhists, witches, therapists,
family, friends, this book has it all. Please read about Deborah's
search for a belief system, the meaning of life and good scones.
You won't be sorry.

— **Colin Mochrie**, star of *Whose Line Is It Anyway?*

With this bold and honest story, Deborah Kimmett's unique voice
is a beacon in today's society where women of a certain age are
rarely seen, let alone heard. Honesty and comedy make for a
powerful combination. As we say in the business, know your audience. Deborah not only knows her audience but she's captured us
brilliantly.

— **Tracy L. Rideout**, former executive producer,
CBC Radio Comedy

Window Shopping for God is a fun page-turner of a book. An
irreverent, poignant, utterly readable and sometimes hysterical
look at the dark, disturbing but mostly hilarious moments in
Deborah Kimmett's life.

— **Mary Walsh**, comedian and co-star of
CBC's *This Hour Has 22 Minutes*

As moving as it is hilarious, Deborah Kimmett's memoir lays bare
the life of a Second City comic. She revels in onstage triumphs
and gets abruptly fired, dates far too many musicians, battles alcoholism, finds sobriety and lurches into motherhood by birthing
two babies in a year, one of them achingly premature. All the while,
Kimmett is looking for God, and we're with her on every step of
her rowdy and riveting quest.

— **Lesley Krueger**, author of *Far Creek Road*

Poignant, vulnerable, and above all, hilarious. Deborah Kimmett walks us through moments big and small with honesty, self-deprecation and a little bit of side-eye. Her ability to make us laugh during some of the hard times in her life might make it easier for us to revisit some of our own hard times with a new perspective that allows for a little more grace and compassion for ourselves and the people around us. Reading *Window Shopping for God* will make you want to sit down with Deb and wax philosophical over a cappuccino...and then make fun of people who wax philosophical.

— **Allison Dore**, host of *The Breakdown* (SiriusXM)
and founder of Howl & Roar Records

Searingly, brutally and hilariously honest!! A beautifully written bittersweet journey celebrating the triumph of spirit. A remarkable read.

— **Ron James**, comedian and bestselling author of
*All Over the Map: Rambles and Ruminations
from the Canadian Road*

Window Shopping for God feels like finding a new friend. It made me cry because I was laughing so hard, and sometimes it just made me cry, in a good way. You'll love this book if you're a recovering Catholic; struggled with addiction; had an undiagnosed brain injury; lost a loved one; worked in comedy; been in therapy; are afraid to start therapy; are a therapist; been a mother; had a mother; had a dog; searched for something called God... what the hell, you'll love this book.

— **Kate Story**, Governor General's Literary Award finalist
and theatre artist

A hilarious, poignant and moving memoir from a very funny lady. *Window Shopping for God* is a must-read for anyone who has ever found themselves searching for meaning, only to discover it hiding in plain sight. I couldn't put it down, and I laughed so hard I cried. This is one of those books that will make people ask, "what ARE you reading???" I highly recommend this book.

— **Colette Baron-Reid**, author, educator and artist

A remarkable book, by a remarkable woman, *Window Shopping for God* will take you on an emotional rollercoaster that ricochets between hilarity and empathy. It is truly heartwarming.

— **David Brady**, film & television producer

If you're looking for God, you might not find what you're looking for in the pages of this book. But if you're looking to tag along for an uproarious spiritual journey of self-revelation, forgiveness and transcendence—wherein the line between truth and memory and outright invention is as inscrutable as an act of divine intervention—this is the book for you. *Window Shopping for God* is daring, innovative and side-splitting.

— **Joel Thomas Hynes**, Governor General's
   Literary Award-winning author

WINDOW SHOPPING FOR GOD

*A Comedian's
Search for Meaning*

DEBORAH KIMMETT

Douglas & McIntyre

Douglas and McIntyre (2013) Ltd.
P.O. Box 219, Madeira Park, BC, VON 2H0
www.douglas-mcintyre.com

Edited by Caroline Skelton
Cover illustration by Heidi Berton
Text design by Libris Simas Ferraz/Onça Publishing
Printed and bound in Canada
Printed on 100% recycled paper

Douglas and McIntyre acknowledges the support of the Canada Council for
the Arts, the Government of Canada, and the Province of British Columbia
through the BC Arts Council.

Library and Archives Canada Cataloguing in Publication
Title: Window shopping for God : a comedian's search for meaning /
    Deborah Kimmett.
Names: Kimmett, Deborah (Deborah Ann), author.
Identifiers: Canadiana (print) 2024030120X | Canadiana (ebook) 20240301374 |
    ISBN 9781771623995 (softcover) | ISBN 9781771624008 (EPUB)
Subjects: LCSH: Kimmett, Deborah (Deborah Ann)—Religion. |
    LCSH: Comedians—Canada—Biography. | LCSH: Spiritual biography—
    Canada. | LCGFT: Autobiographies.
Classification: LCC BL73.K56 A3 2024 | DDC 204.092—dc23

window shopping for God
1.   the activity of looking for *gods* in holy places,
      without ever intending to buy anything.

To my lovely brother.

CONTENTS

Inventing God

Baptism by Fire

The Goldman Sessions

Bardos

Afterlife

AUTHOR'S NOTE

There are two kinds of memories. There is the memory of what you thought happened and then there are the stories you tell about the memory that you thought happened. The stories here are both. They all are true, but as my brother Kevin said, they have lost no flavour in the retelling. In some cases the names have been changed to protect privacy, and timelines and conversations have been altered and reconstructed for narrative reasons, but I did stay faithful to the emotional truth. Unless there was an opportunity to tell a really good joke.

PREACHERMAN

"DO YOU BELIEVE IN GOD?" The first day I met the man called Preacherman, I was sitting in front of the scone place at St. Clair and Christie as he preached the word of God. That's if God was having a really bad day. He stood on his crate, impeccably groomed. He wore a beige cashmere coat—quite fancy for a street preacher—and a fedora with a black scarf under his hat to keep his head warm. Up on his crate, he loomed large to passersby.

Sitting there eating my scone, I had so many questions. *What was the first day you decided to come out to the street and preach? Has your yelling converted one single person? And why do you never see a woman standing out here on soapboxes?*

It was 2014, and I was glad to be back in the city, in the thick of things. I had my new old dog, Gus—a fourteen-year-old shih tzu with a severe underbite that made him look like Marlon Brando in *The Godfather*, "I'm gonna make him an offer he can't refuse."

I'd lived in both city and country settings for equal amounts of time. I grew up in a small town, moved to the big city, back to live on a small island near Kingston, and then returned to the city again. I loved living in every one of those settings until the moment I didn't. One morning, I'd wake up to a wind blowing in off the lake and I'd start building a case against the place and the people. Soon, I'd be gone again.

I moved back to Toronto a few months after I found out my brother Kevin was sick. I had been perfectly happy living in the woods with twelve acres of forest behind me, the Cataraqui Trail to walk on daily and Varty Lake nearby for daily dips in the summer. Within a few months of receiving the bad news, I began to tell everybody that I hated trees and my landlord smoked on the back porch. To top it off, the long driveway was never plowed, and I was constantly snowed in. I only got snowed in once, but I was making my case to pack up and go. I didn't think there was any connection between Kevin's impending death and my impulse to move yet again. I just gave my notice, packed up Gus and went to Toronto—the opposite direction of Ottawa, where Kevin lived. He had his own family to take care of him, so it wasn't that. I wasn't running away either. I've lived long enough to know you can't outrun trouble. Trouble knows your forwarding address and will be snoring in the spare bedroom before you've unpacked the U-Haul. And I wasn't leaving because I was afraid. Sick people have never frightened me. I had been sick as a kid, and it had granted me some strange superpower that meant I knew what to say when people were in crisis or in life-and-death situations. Or maybe it was because I had died so many times on stage.

I wasn't running away as much as I was running toward a life I had given up years before. We had left the city when my kids were young, and even though I loved living out in the middle of nowhere, I wanted to go back and explore some still unrealized parts of myself before it was too late.

On my fiftieth birthday, my Aunt Mary sent me a card that said, "Now that you're fifty, the days will drag, and the weeks will fly by. Happy Birthday." With a wish like that, there should've been money in the card. But she was right. Those past nine years had

2

gone somewhere, and it seemed like every time I looked up it was Thursday.

I packed up the dog and rented a spot one block west of bougie and one block east of despair, hoping an urban setting would give me one more kick at the can. Larger audiences and more auditions for TV.

Maybe the pursuit of my abandoned dreams was just my own personal shell game, but one thing was for sure: nothing new was going to happen to me when I was out in the middle of the woods, sitting on my porch swing, chewing a piece of grass.

Despite my protests to the contrary, my country friends thought I was making a terrible mistake. "Everyone is trying to get out of Toronto, and you are trying to get back in," they said.

But I had tried to make living in the country work. I even tried to buy a mobile home. I reasoned it cost so little I could pay cash, live in a trailer park on weekends and have a flat in the city. The best of both worlds, I said. You're not a mobile home person, friends said. You never know, I might be a mobile home kind of person, I said. It was the same lie I told myself about camping. I could be a camping person if it wasn't for the sleeping outdoors part, and the mosquitoes part, and the communal bathroom part.

I had gone quite far along in the process; put down the deposit and signed on the dotted line, and I was about to pick up the keys when I noticed the sign above the entrance to the park. A sign I swear hadn't been there two days before: "Welcome to Richmond Retirement Park." Where did that sign come from? It was as if the word *retirement* had stars around it like this was a country everyone wanted to enter. It might as well have said, "Welcome to Death Row" because I cried out to Gus, "This cannot be how my life ends. In a trailer park?" I could just see the headline in our local rag, the *Napanee Beaver*: "Debbie Kimmett ended up exactly where she started." Up until that moment, neither Gus nor I had any idea I felt so negative about retirement or trailer parks. But there we were. I went from *living in a mobile home is an excellent idea* to *what the hell was I thinking* in the space of about ten minutes. I withdrew the offer on the spot, cut my losses, packed our bags and moved back to the city.

As I barrelled down the highway with the shih tzu on my lap, I reviewed the close call: "Thank God I saw the sign when I did. Otherwise, where would we be, Gus? One step closer to death, that's where. I think that old guy driving by on a golf buggy might have been the Grim Reaper."

Whenever you start over, everything is shiny and new—worthy of a status update on Facebook. A short period when you look at even the most arcane things with the eyes of a tourist. *Did you see that rock? That rock is historical. Did you know our founding forefathers rolled that rock up here from the States?* It's a short window of time before your eyes will adjust to the view and soon even the most beautiful surroundings will become wallpaper, pasted onto the background that you walk by on your way to work.

It had been years since I'd lived in an apartment building, smelling other people's dinners. Hearing people partying and crying babies squawking at all hours of the day. All that noise was why I had left the city the first time. But all wasn't serene in the country either: there, it was the sound of coyotes killing their prey that kept me up. Most nights it sounded like Khandar out there. After living in the wilderness for nearly twelve years, I decided that if I were going to wake up before dawn, I'd rather it be from the sound of human beings.

Back in Toronto, I was happy to hear people shutting apartment doors, going to work in the morning; at night, screaming soccer fans honking horns when their team won the cup, and rap music pumping from cars in the heat of the summer. I didn't even mind fire engines racing by at three in the morning. All that urban energy made me feel like at any moment something could happen.

Within days, I knew everyone in the neighbourhood. I've retained the small-town quality of talking to everybody that has a minute to spare, even the ones who don't. Over the years, I've developed a collection of guaranteed icebreakers: "Can I just say? Your dog is the cutest. What kind is it? A lab mix? Gorgeous. By the way, your shoelace is untied. I don't want you to trip over your feet."

I inherited this quality from my dad. He used to drive downtown waving at everybody like he was the mayor of Napanee. It would take him a couple hours to walk a block from the bank to his van. When he went to the local dump, he'd be gone all afternoon. No matter what a person's station in life, after a ten-minute conversation with my father, they'd tell him their entire life story. Their wife's name, that their kids don't come home much anymore and how their sister hates her boss. Dad had a face that made people think he cared about them. He'd never say much but a silent man often appears wiser than he is. He would nod and laugh in the right places, and more importantly, he'd follow it up with action. He'd do anything for anybody. Drive a hitchhiker to his destination, pick a guy up from jail. Once, he followed a complete stranger home and fixed their broken toilet.

For the most part, people want to talk to me as well. It's something about my face. That wholesome, well-fed farm face; a face that looks like I drink a lot of cow's milk. A face that, when I was younger, I had tried to contour out of existence.

Right on cue, Preacherman interrupted my musings and yelled again, like maybe half the neighbourhood hadn't heard his question the first time. "I SAID DO YOU BELIEVE IN ONE TRUE GOD?" I know this was likely a rhetorical question, but I found myself thinking about it—although the word "God" is the one I yell out when I stub my toe in the middle of the night.

I'd spent fifty years wrestling with that three-letter word. But it sounded like the God he was selling would have to be small enough to fit inside the lyrics of a country music song.

Let's pretend for a second that I did answer him and say indeed I do believe in the one true God. How would that go? *Would your God be the same as mine? Are you assuming I believe in Jesus's dad? Or Allah? Or Yahweh? Tell me, sir: What sort of one true God are you looking for?*

Over my lifetime, I'd bowed down at the feet of them all. Jesus, Buddha, Kali, Krishna. The real gods and the false. Booze, men, and Facebook. I had danced with witches, whirled with Sufis and explored *The Power of Now* like there is no tomorrow. After all that time and money, you'd think that Amazon would've delivered me a deity in which I could believe with complete certainty, but it had not. And any faith I had cobbled together over my life had been waning, ever since my brother was diagnosed with a glioblastoma tumour. Which is not one of *those* tumours. Not a my-second-cousin-twice-removed-had-a-tumour-and-drank-sheep-urine-and-got-it-cut-out-and-now-she's-fine tumours.

A GB tumour is aggressive. It doesn't care about anyone's spiritual credentials. It was like the landlord had given him notice and developers were coming in and tearing the building down. We could beg and plead and say he'd been a good tenant, but that kind of tumour doesn't care. The wrecking ball was coming. My brother, who had always believed in the one true God, had less than a year to live.

But when a man on a soapbox screams at you, you know there is no point in giving him your spiritual resumé, because you can't convince a zealot of a god-dang thing.

LOSING
MY
RELIGION

NO LONGER CATHOLIC

"I'm no longer Catholic,**"** I mumbled as I came to. I'd been on a rip the night before.

My mother was standing over me in my childhood bedroom, yelling, "Get out of bed right this minute and get to Mass!" Her eyes bore down on me like Gary Cooper's in *High Noon* as she tried to bully me into meeting my Sunday obligation. That was what church was—an obligation. No matter where you were in the world, you needed to hunt down Mass schedules in the area and get to church sometime between Saturday and Sunday evenings. I was twenty-one years old, going to college, and except when I was home for the weekend, I had given up on church. A fact I had not told my mother yet. I opened one eye and saw the morning sun bounce off her Vatican special-edition rosary beads.

My mother wondered what had happened to the faithful child I was, who, at one time, couldn't wait to go to Mass. The child who loved the smell of the incense that the priest shook over the congregation, practically choking us out. I sniffed the varnished wood every time I kneeled down. My immediate family sometimes went to Mass on Saturday night, but my grandparents were there every Sunday. Grandpa would stand at the back with the men in dark

11

suits, ready to take up the collection plate. Their suits smelled like moth balls and Aqua Velva aftershave and they looked like bodyguards ready to block any recalcitrant teenagers trying to escape before Communion. Grandma smelled like Pepsodent tooth powder and wore wildly coloured hot pants with dark pantyhose underneath and white plastic shoes. She would let me sit in her regular spot and would make sassy comments all through Mass. When I hushed her, she'd snarl, "I've prayed enough for a hundred lifetimes." This laissez-faire attitude concerned me so much, I prayed even more adamantly.

I believed the prayers that the priest and congregation recited during Mass would transform the host into Christ's body. I'm not speaking metaphorically here. I thought the vessel was empty at the beginning of Mass, and if we stood, sat, kneeled in the right order, and didn't tell off-colour jokes like Grandma, the wafers would magically drop from the sky into the chalice.

I believed in transubstantiation and Santa until I was of an embarrassing age. "A magical thinker" is what psychologists would eventually call it. The type of kid who, every year on my birthday, was convinced my family would jump out from behind the furniture to give me a surprise party. I also had blind faith that if I prayed hard enough, I'd be cured of the psoriasis that covered most of my body. My family took me to dermatologists, but they also took me to shrines. Some people go to their cottage in the summer, but I was busy touring the shrine circuit, praying for smooth skin. From St. Anne's in Montreal to Midland where Father Brébeuf was martyred, I went to them all, mostly with my grandparents. The most popular shrine they frequented was outside Eganville, which we visited in mid-August when it was hotter than the hub of hell. It was a preview of what the temperature would be if you let up on your prayers for even a second. In a huge open field with no trees, I'd genuflect before many porcelain saints in the midday sun, moving my way around the rosary beads as I did the Stations of the Cross. If I did enough prostrations, perhaps psoriatic plaques would be left behind on the altar as proof of my devotion. Even though all I got for my efforts was heatstroke and maybe a quick swim in a creek on the ride home, my faith never wavered that a miracle was around the next corner.

I performed these rituals in the hope that one day I would be seen as special in the eyes of our Lord, and my mother. You think genuflecting at shrines was where this ended? I also produced elaborate Christmas concerts as a tribute to the birth of the baby Jesus. As the self-appointed director, writer, producer and star of these productions, my directorial style mimicked Francis Ford Coppola in his *Apocalypse Now* phase. The rehearsals were fraught with a diva's emotions. Many a night, my five brothers and sisters were downstairs in the rec room rehearsing, with me screaming, "If you guys don't get this right, Mom and Dad will walk out!" to which my sister Karen, aka the Virgin Mary, would smugly retort, "They live here. Where are they going to go? Upstairs?" She almost got recast as the Third Wise Man for that crack.

There had been too many productions where the Virgin just sat there looking beatific, so I rewrote the stable scene from a feminist perspective. As the plastic shower curtain opened, my sister acted out a homebirth, complete with labour pains, while Alice Cooper's "Only Women Bleed" blasted from the cassette tape deck. When she was about ten centimetres dilated, she pushed the baby Jesus out from between her legs.

My two-year-old brother crawled out from under her skirt and said, "Me no like sandals." Then he went and sat on my mother's lap. My parents laughed so hard; Dad had to take off his glasses to wipe away the tears. Despite all of this, they didn't walk out, but I almost did. I began crying and screaming that everybody was ruining my creative vision. Then my mother, in that loving way she had, said, "For God's sake, stop your bleating and finish this up so we can have a snack." Many directors afterward would say the same thing to me. After Mary retreated, obviously spent from her lengthy stable delivery, I once again took centre stage. My bangs hung in front of my eyes as I strummed the guitar, singing, It's Good News week ... someone's dropped a bomb somewhere ... contaminating the atmosphere" (from the song by the Hedgehoppers Anonymous) I sang in the key of off, and my mother took a moment to change Jesus's diaper while Dad nodded off in his La-Z-Boy.

I had given Catholicism a good run. But slowly, I had put two and two together. In the same year I discovered there was no Santa, I had found out that the nuns baked the hosts. Everyone else got that memo but me. When I told Mom I thought that we prayed hard and the Communion appeared, she looked at me. "Do you have a screw loose?" she said. "They are baked in Kingston at the convent and brought to the church on Sunday." What was the point in all that praying if the nuns had already baked the hosts? Where was the magic there? That was the beginning of the end. Yes, I kept blessing myself when I drove by a Catholic church, pinning saints' medals to my bra during exam time and dropping to my knees when I thought I was pregnant, but that was not faith as much as it was early signs of OCD.

On that fateful hungover morning, I was sick and tired of praying to dour-looking saints with glassed-over eyes that followed you around the room; sick of all the kneeling, genuflecting; and most of all, I was sick of this woman I called mother trying to guilt me to get up and go to Mass.

As Mom's face came into focus, I saw her shaking her head like a horse does when someone tries to force a bit into its mouth.

"What did you say?"

"I said I'm no longer Catholic."

"What?"

"I am not a Catholic anymore!" *God, is the woman deaf?*

"Get up out of that bed and get to Mass before I crucify you."

The threat of crucifixion would be all the motivation needed for most kids to get up and get going, but it didn't faze me. Nailing me to a cross in the afternoon sun had been her go-to threat since I was a young child. "Clean that bedroom of yours before I crucify you." "Eat your peas before I crucify you." Sometimes, when she was furious, she'd even describe how she was going to do it: "If you don't get up off that couch and help me do the dishes, I'm going to nail your hands and feet to the clothesline pole in the backyard for all the neighbours to see." I knew it was a bogus threat. My mother wouldn't even hang her underpants on the clothesline in case people guessed her bra size. She was hardly going to hang me or any one of us up in the backyard for all the neighbours to see.

I peeked my head out from under the covers and mumbled, "If you crucify me, how am I going to be able to go to Mass?" She closed her mouth, made her lips lie flat, and suddenly a high-pitched sound escaped from them. She sounded like a balloon losing air. As one hand swatted at me, the other yanked the covers off me. I still had on my bra and my day-of-the-week underpants. But they were the wrong day. Where had Friday and Saturday gone? And why was I only wearing one knee-high hose and one high-heeled shoe?

My mother zeroed in on the shoe covered in mud. "Hell and damnation. Do you think you're having fun?"

Pretty sure this was a rhetorical question, I pulled the covers back over my head, almost asphyxiating myself with my tequila breath.

"Take your damn shoes off when you go to bed at night." Then she slammed the door until the frame shook on its hinges. When I thought it was safe, I poked my head out from under the covers just as the door swung open again and she fired one more shot: "You can't stop being Catholic. You were born Catholic. You will die

Catholic." There it was—the curse. The curse I would try to out-run for the next thirty years, because you don't quit that religion. Catholicism is like the Hotel California—you can check out, but you can never leave.

At the time, I thought I was the only one having these kinds of interactions with their Catholic mothers. I didn't realize that I was part of an entire generation letting go of the traditional religions for more secular faiths. For many in my generation, our needs of shelter and food were met so we had enough time to explore meaning. People without food in their bellies are not reflecting on what their life journey is. But I was too busy drinking and thinking I was a rebel to know I was part of the cultural zeitgeist.

While I was feeling like a female Kant, Eastern philosophies washed over the Pacific and assimilated themselves into every corner of Canadian culture. Where I grew up, two hours east of Toronto in the small town of Napanee, the only Eastern influence was the Chinese restaurant—the New Yorker Café, which served frozen egg rolls. Suddenly, Asian restaurants sprung up on every corner, and we began eating Phad Thai and sushi like we had finally discovered the meaning of life. In Toronto, I used to go to Kensington Market and wear kimonos to eat gado-gado at the BamBoo Club on Queen Street West.

I stopped saying the rosary but I wore the beads as a necklace, reducing my Catholic upbringing to an accessory.

Growing up in Napanee, there were three choices: Catholic or Protestant or Jewish. But before long, religion became an inter-national all-you-can-eat buffet.

It was not until the past few years that I realized how much the way we worship has changed since I grew up. A few years back, I was sitting in a café and I looked over and saw a Chinese woman next to me slurping foam on her latte while she, the newly minted Christian, had crawled inside the New Testament. I, an ex-Catholic, was sipping green tea and reading *The Tibetan Book of the Dead*—a detailed outline of how to stay conscious as you die so you won't get caught by the Hungry Ghosts. Heady stuff. Both of us sat there reading two of the harshest books ever printed, because when you abandon your original faith, you often embrace another that is just as harsh as the one you left.

When the newly minted Christian saw my choice of books, the woman smiled and said, "Hey look at us. We did a faith swap." We chatted for a bit and then looked up at the menu, confiding in each other that we had no idea what a Vietnamese coffee would taste like.

NEAR-DEATH EXPERIENCE

Years before, I fell off my bike and nearly died.

I am not sure if it would qualify as a near-death experience in TV terms. I didn't have family members come from the other side to greet me. No angels appeared to take me for Jell-O in the afterlife cafeteria.

But when I returned to the land of the living, I had changed. I came back knowing something most teenagers don't know: I knew death and life walked side by side. Death wasn't something that just happened to old people. It was not way over there. It was close. A line you could cross in a millisecond.

One minute you were here, and the next, you were not.

It had been one of those perfect summer evenings. We were having a picnic at the house of my mom's friend, who lived on a county road south of Napanee. The fields were yellow with canola. They called it rapeseed back then—an unfortunate name for such a beautiful yellow. I was on my bike, pedalling like the devil. I remember my long blond hair blowing in the wind. I was ahead of the kids in the line of cyclists. The last thing I recall was gripping the Mustang handle bars, boasting to my sister, who was well behind me on her bike, about how fast I was going.

I woke up four days later—in the hospital—not recalling the in-between. I heard later that Dad got me into the back of the station wagon and I threw up all the way to the hospital. None of the emergency doctors took my condition seriously. Finally, Aunty D, Mom's sister and a mother of eight, stepped up and said, "Get a doctor in here right now, or there will be hell to pay." Within minutes, a surgeon miraculously appeared and said, "Get this girl to the operating room."

I had a sub-cranial bleed—a broken blood vessel—pushing against my brain, making me slur my words and dribble soup down my chin. When I came to, my eyes were swollen shut. Blood pooled around my eyes, which was part of the routine healing. Because they had to check my pupils every hour, I received no pain meds. My head felt like it was splitting in two. As I surfaced, I heard flies buzzing. As I squinted through my swollen eyes, I saw shadows of a small group standing around me. Mom and Dad for sure, but the faces and names of the rest of the group escaped me. I could hear them saying the rosary. Waking up to people standing over your bed praying is not comforting at all. I was sure I was dead. Then a black shadow bent in, with a cigarette-smelling thumb soaked in oil, and this greasy digit painted the sign of the cross on my forehead. The thumb belonged to the parish priest, Father O'Neill—a lovely man with a nasal voice that tortured us all with his dry whiny sermons every Sunday. He leaned over the bed and said, "Welcome back. God saved you for a reason." Then he left, not explaining what that reason was.

I was a teenager, so I wasn't allowed on the pediatric floor. I had been put on the cardiac wing in a private room, with no buzzer to push for help. There was a bell on my dinner tray I was supposed to ring should I need to be taken to the bathroom. But after ringing it several times to no avail, I finally walked down the hall to the bathroom on my own. When I returned to my room, I saw a bag taped to the bottom of the bed. When I looked in, I found it was full of hair.

Why did they put hair in a bag? I instinctively reached for my head, swaddled in white cloth, and slowly began to realize that underneath the bandages, I was bald.

What am I supposed to do with the hair in the bag? Make a hairpiece from it? Knit it into a sweater?

The accident was profitable. I cleaned up financially: my family gave me cards and toys and money—forty-two dollars to be exact. Two dollars more than I would've made had I continued to babysit the two boys down the road. And now I didn't have to toilet train the youngest one.

Until my brother Kevin called it a brain injury, it never occurred to me that this was what happened to me. After the accident, if someone even suggested that what I had was a brain injury, my mother would bend over backward to reassure them that I was completely "normal" because it was only a "head injury." Head, brain, completely different things.

Except for a future lifetime hatred of cycling, no long-term damage was done, but I felt far from normal. Before the accident, I was Debbie Ann Kimmett, who had a full head of beautiful blond hair. After the accident, I was bald Debi with an *i* who was about to enter Grade Nine. It was 1970, and Sinéad O'Connor hadn't arrived on the scene, so bald heads weren't acceptable fashion statements. If this had happened today, other kids would have shaved their heads in solidarity. They would have painted henna designs on my bald pate. Someone would have started a GoFundMe. No one made a fuss or guided me. God was testing me, but for what I didn't know.

My mother and I went shopping for my new head of hair at Sears. She wanted me to go with something short and perky—a reasonable request if I was playing the mom on *The Partridge*

Family. But before the accident, I had had hair down past my shoulders, so I wanted a wig that reminded me of that gal. After much deliberation, I chose a long ash-blond polyester wig. Natural hair wasn't in our price point. For years, I remembered it as a bouffant, a cross between what Farrah Fawcett and Dolly Parton would wear. But when I saw the picture recently, I realized the look was less country and more secretarial school.

I was bald so I wasn't going to model it out in the aisle with all the customers so I went into the change room. When I came out a few moments later mom gasped, "Jesus, Mary and Joseph. Look at that monstrosity. You're going to stick out like a sore thumb." (It was ironic that less than a week later, she suggested I wear my brother's hockey helmet to the Napanee Fair because she didn't want me to hurt my head on the Tilt-A-Whirl.) She let me get the wig but would only pay for half of it. "That eye sore is double what the pixie cut is." I paid with it from the money I got from the accident.

Then the eye sore and I headed off to Grade Nine.

Every time he saw me at school, my goof ball neighbour would ask me the same question: "Is that a wig you are wearing, Debi Kimmett?" And, every single day, I would lie and say, "No. No. Dean, this is not a wig." I'd quickly place both my hands on my head and serpentine down the hallways, so neither he nor any of the other idiots in high school would pull it off. Then, I'd brace for the bus ride home.

School buses are a living hell at the best of times. Let's put thirty kids in a yellow death trap with no seatbelts, then hire a person for minimum wage who can never find any of the familiar landmarks—a frazzled woman, barrelling up the 401, casually hunched over the wheel, yelling to the back of the bus, "Where is the CN Tower exactly?" Every day, a kid named Barry (he had a twin called Harry—it appeared they shared the same brain) would

21

crawl up behind me, grab for my wig and stop just short of touching me, then run to the back of the bus, laughing with his crew of thick necks. I rode home with both hands over my head.

It was a confusing time. On the one hand, I liked boys and wanted their attention. But on the other hand, I didn't want it from the Barrys of the world. It was Mike K from homeroom I wanted. He was a Kennard. I was Kimmett. Our lockers were next to each other and just him turning the cylinders left then right on his silver lock made me break out in a full sweat.

Despite our K connection, Mike never spoke to me. Not once in the entire year. He was either introverted or stoned. Maybe both. Most days during the morning announcements, he'd squeeze white glue onto his palm to watch it dry. He had dark, long shoulder-length hair, which he was always chewing on; a wet lock curled around his face to his mouth, which made him even more attractive. He was all I thought about. In the bathroom at school, I'd look in the mirror and practice saying hello. *Hi, Mike. Hello, Michael. Hey, M.* But I never managed to emit more than a squeak when he stood next to me.

I fantasized that he and I were making out in the back of his car. (He was only in Grade Nine and didn't even drive yet, but fantasies don't require learner's permits.) As we were hugging and kissing with his fingers running through my wig, he would accidentally pull it off and reveal my bald head. In this fantasy, Mike did not mind my stubble. He was not shallow like most guys. He looked at that beautiful bald head of mine and asked me to the prom. In turn, I made a macramé halter top for myself, and for him, a matching cowboy vest. We married at the Sadie Hawkins Dance, and got him off "the drugs," and he fought me on it, but when he became a famous hockey player for the NHL, I was the first person he thanked when he bowed his head before every game: "Thank you, God, for Debbie Kimmett. She saved my life."

From the get-go, I was saving an imaginary boyfriend from drug addiction.

Mike wasn't interested in me saving him because he didn't know I was alive. If there were a Grade Nine handbook it would tell you the Mike Ks of the world never know you are alive. Even though I prayed faithfully, God didn't give me the cute guy. In my nightly prayers, I begged God for my hair to grow back faster than everyone else's: *I know you created hair to grow a quarter inch a month, but please, please let mine grow an inch a month.* Every morning, I checked the mirror to see if I had grown my blond locks again, and every morning it was still the same stubble. God also took away the blond and made me a brunette. God didn't give me any special treatment, and neither did anyone else.

Having a brain bleed didn't get me out of housework: I had to vacuum, do the dishes and take care of the little kids. Because there were six of us, my parents had little, if any, time to coddle me. We said the rosary every night and ripped off a stream of special intentions for children of war and single mothers who wanted to have an abortion, but I don't recall my bald head getting as much as an honourable mention. I donned my wig and carried on.

The only person who understood my hair trouble was Grandma Brady—an outlier of a woman—who besides wearing short shorts to Mass, wore a wig: a black candy floss postiche, ratted up so high it teetered when she walked. For years she had kept the grey away by dying her hair with a temporary black spray. As a blonde, you didn't dare borrow her hairbrush or you'd go home looking like a zebra. Finally, she got sick of the bother involved in covering the roots and bought several cheap wigs from Woolworths. If you went into her closet, you would see wig heads staring at you. When she saw me tugging at mine, she said, "It looks fine."

"Mom thinks it's too much."

To Grandma Brady, my wig was not too much at all. She felt it wasn't quite enough. In fact, she thought I could use a little volume. She'd stand over me, ratting it out, spraying hairspray.

When I stayed overnight, sometimes we'd play hair salon. One night, while I sat with a toque on, and she teased out my hair as it sat on the styrofoam head, I told her about Barry, and she asked what I was going to do about it. I said I thought God was testing me to rise above the situation and that I was praying for Barry. She shook her head. "Prayer doesn't work in this situation. You know why? Because men do whatever they like. They are arseholes. Did I ever tell you that?"

"Yes, you've mentioned that." All she ever did was tell me all men were arseholes, and so did her daughters. Grandma thought her husband was one. As well as most of her sons. And for sure all her sons-in-law. Since men did what they liked, they needed to be put in their place. "Praying for arseholes is pointless. Do you know what I believe? God helps those who help themselves!"

"What should I do?"

"The first thing you need is a scarf." She pulled a purple scarf from her multicolour collection of cheap Woolworths scarves, tied it around the back of my head, then took the two ends, tied them under my chin, and told me to hold on tight. "When that little bastard goes to pull your wig off, you hold the scarf tight." Then she winked. "We are just two girls trying to beat the men at their own game."

I had no idea what game we were beating them at, but the following Monday, the wig and I got back on the bus along with Grandma's "go big or stay home" fashion tips. I entered the bus in her purple hot pants, black plastic boots and mascara so thickly spread on it looked like ants were crawling under my eyes. I sat down, grabbed the tails of the scarf, and tied them under my chin. Barry snuck up behind me. I felt his hand nearing my head, so

I turned to him and said, "Can I help you?" Then I winked as Grandma had, and he turned red and suddenly he grabbed he bent over and grabbed his crotch. I don't know why he was skulking back to his seat with his hands between his legs but I felt something strange and powerful, like I had just discovered fire. Or developed a superpower that could reduce men to ashes.

SATAN IN MY UNDERPANTS

Despite all the prayers for my return to health after the accident, no one thought to pray for me to stay blond. Thankfully, Sun-In came out on the market the same year as Bonne Bell lip gloss. With all these excellent makeup products, I should've been able to relax and get on with the usual humiliations of high school. But it wasn't just my hair that came in darker than ever; so did my mood. My worry got turned up a notch.

I was blindsided by *The Exorcist*. This cult classic stars Linda Blair, whose character is possessed by a demon voiced by Mercedes McCambridge. I hadn't even seen the movie, only read about it in the *National Enquirer* when I visited a friend whose mother read such rags. *National Enquirer* claimed that since the movie had debuted, exorcisms in the U.S. were at an all-time high for teenage girls.

In what would now be considered obsessive-compulsive disorder, I became consumed with the idea that the devil would take over my soul. I was convinced that I was going to be the target of Satanic possession. And yes, Satan was a "he." If God was male, then obviously the Lord of the Underworld was too. A female demon would still only hit her head on the glass ceiling. Or was it a gas ceiling? I would be okay during the day and at bedtime fall asleep quickly; then I'd bolt forth from a dead sleep, terrified that Satan would make his move while I slumbered. The first time this happened, I was staying with my grandparents. In the middle of the night, I woke up with a start. Even before *The Exorcist*, the quiet at their farm unnerved me. Still enough that you could hear the cows chewing cud in the field. As I lay in bed looking out the window, the scene was bucolic, like an Alex Colville painting, rich blues with a moon so full it ached. The cattle lay still, poetically oblivious to their fate.

Grandpa and Grandma had separate bedrooms—"I don't need that one bumping his manhood up against me in the middle of the night"—and as they snored in unison, in surround sound, one thought tortured me: What if when I fell asleep, Satan made his move and crawled into my underpants, then in an altered state, I murdered my grandparents? Once that thought took hold, I couldn't remove it. I stayed on guard till morning.

I quickly stopped staying overnight, and I began going to confession once or twice a week. I had recited some version of the same three sins since I was six years old. "Bless me, Father. I've lied to my parents; I hit my brothers; I stole candy from my sister's Easter basket." But now I confessed my lack of faith and my worry. Still, I couldn't mention demonic possession. The priest was a nice guy. He and Dad were on the cemetery committee together. What would he think of me if I started chatting about exorcisms?

After several confessions, the best I could do was blurt out that I had some dark thoughts. "Dark thoughts?"

"Yes."

"Like?

"Like really dark thoughts."

"Like despair?"

"Yup. Sure." *Why not?*

"You have despair. Despair is a sin."

He told me to say three Hail Marys. I was already saying enough Hail Marys to send despair into the middle of next week, and it wasn't having any effect. I left the confessional knowing I was wrestling the darkness on my own.

I began a repetitive nightly ritual. First, I pinned saints' medals to my undershirts, then I started to wear two pairs of underpants under my pajamas. Maybe underpants couldn't stop Satan, but they might slow him down a bit. Then I'd get into bed and repeatedly recite the rosary, eventually giving me calluses on my thumb and index fingers. Some nights I'd pass out from sheer exhaustion, but I'd always wake up around one in the morning, which, according to the *National Enquirer*, was Satan's witching hour.

During these nightly walkabouts, I'd find my dad lying on the floor, cracking his knees in the living room. He was a long-legged man with no meat on his bones, so his joints constantly ached. Work was his religion. Besides a full-time job, he always worked about three side hustles to stay afloat with six kids. Dad's legs and mind were restless, so he'd lie on the floor and settle the world's problems way into the wee hours.

No one could bring a lump to my throat faster than my father. He was such a great guy, and everyone loved him. There he was on the floor, alone. *Poor Dad, all alone.* Not once did it occur to me that the middle of the night was the only time when he could have a thought for himself. I'd sit on the La-Z-Boy and stare at him. His arm bent across his eyes, and without moving a muscle, he'd ask, "You got squirrels in the attic?" He asked it in a way that implied he, at times in his life, had had the same rodents as me.

"I can't sleep."

"What's on your mind?"

Dad, I think Satan can crawl into my underpants, and if he did, I could kill people. I couldn't say that. Not to Dad. When I told him I had a training bra, he wouldn't let me crawl on his lap after, so I couldn't possibly mention I feared Satan crawling into my under-pants when Dad was there in *his* underpants. No, not boxer shorts, but underpants. All dads of the '60s walked around unabashedly in those kinds of underpants. "I am just worried about stuff."

And he said what every dad has said since the beginning of time, "What would you have to worry about?"

Telling a worrywart not to worry only makes things worse. There was plenty to worry about. Dad was born a Protestant, and even though he converted to Catholicism when he and my mom decided to get married, he really had no idea how powerful Satan could be. He went to church, but he napped throughout most of the sermon. Mom would poke him and, after the service, apolo-gize to the priest, but Father O'Neill loved my dad. "Well, Jim must have a clean conscience if he can nod off like that." Dad was exhausted from all the jobs he had, but he'd always wake up in time to take up the collection. He was part of the parish council, attended the church socials and sat on every parish committee. Maybe it was because he was religious, or maybe he just wanted to avoid putting the kids to bed.

Our middle-of-the-night chats were the only quality time we ever had together. During my nightly excursions, he'd read me excerpts from Norman Vincent Peale's *The Power of Positive Thinking: A Practical Guide to Mastering the Problems of Everyday Living*.

One of the stories in the book was about a woman whose husband went out every night to the bar while she sat home alone, wishing he loved her more. When she went to see Norman Vincent Peale, he told her she needed to visualize your husband enjoying her and staying home. She returned home and started saying positive things repeatedly, imagining that her man was next to her in his rocking chair. She even went so far as to create imagin-ary loving conversations—the kind they had when they were first in love. Then one night, lo and behold, he stayed home, and that began the next chapter in their very successful marriage.

I read a couple of chapters on my own and began repeating positive things too. *I will sleep well tonight. I won't think of Satan.* The more I chanted, the more the wicked thoughts took hold. Norman Vincent Peale wasn't Catholic. *Maybe Norman Vincent Peale is one of Satan's go-to guys.*

"Get in bed with your mother," Dad would say. I'd crawl in beside her. I loved my mother best when she was sleeping. All the anger had drained away. She was so still I'd move close to her face to see if she was breathing. After a few nights of these nocturnal visits, she opened one eye and said, "I swear to God; you need to stop this nonsense."

She had no clue what nonsense I had going on in my head, but her annoyance slapped me into sleep. In the night, she'd sometimes reach her hand out and tap me on the side of my stomach, and I'd snuggle next to her. I felt safe. For if anyone could ward off Satan, it would be my mother. And God help any demon that interrupted her sleep. I could just hear her rebuking him: "What are you doing lurking around, at this time of night with all those serpents? Go lie down."

I continued sleeping with her on and off for several weeks until one morning in early spring, I awoke to her standing over me, shaking her head. "You've got to stop doing this or we're going to take you to a psychiatrist."

"Really? I *get* to go to a psychiatrist?" *Oh God, I'd kill for a psychiatrist.*

"No, not *really*. I don't have time to be trotting you off to some head doctor. Smarten up."

But instead, she took me to Sears and bought me store-bought clothes: jeans and a half-baby-blue, half-pink fuzzy top. I knew she was worried about me because I never got store-bought anything: we didn't have the money. We ate in the Sears cafeteria, and I had a big plate of sloppy joes, which I had only sampled once, at Grandma Kimmett's.

Perhaps it was our mother-daughter shop, or that we changed to daylight saving time, but I began to feel better. It was May and I walked downtown with my friends. The air was damp and a couple of guys we didn't know in a souped-up greaseball car pulled up and asked, "You want to drive around?" We nodded and jumped in, and after a few laps around Napanee, one of the boys asked me to the formal dance at our high school.

Mom made me a blue satin dress from scratch, and I acted like I didn't like it, but I thought it was beautiful. It looked like satin sheets had been removed from a waterbed and were draped over my nubile seventeen-year-old body. The boy arrived and pinned a corsage near my right breast. Mom was making such a fuss, taking pictures, and Dad was saying classic father things like, "Don't you dare put your banana in her lunchbox." When we got to the car, the boy pulled out a mickey of lemon gin, and I'd chugged about a third of it when he said, "That was for all of us to share." By the time I got to the dance, all thoughts of Satan were gone.

Under the disco ball, the '70s music blaring, I felt like myself for the first time. I was Debbie Ann Kimmett, a sex kitten whose hair looked like a wind machine was following her around wherever she went. That night, I became very musical. I danced, shaking my fists up and down like a go-go girl, and, if I remember correctly, some of the cool kids from the hockey team gathered around and cheered me on.

When the dance was over, the boy drove me down to the end of a dark road and we alternated between making out and puking. First, him. Then, me. I'd chew gum, reapply peach Bonne Bell lip gloss, and we'd begin kissing again. I didn't want to get in trouble, so I insisted he and his friend drop me off at the corner of our road, and I tiptoed home past the neighbours' houses with my shoes in my hands.

Scared I'd run into Dad and Norman Vincent Peale, I climbed in my basement bedroom window, fell on my sister's bed, and threw up all night. When I got up the next day, my mother said, "Were you drinking last night?"

"Absolutely not." All teenagers think they've pulled the wool over their parents' eyes, so I was convinced she believed me.

Did she know what I would eventually become? Years later, I realized she knew more than she let on. When my mother had to go into the nursing home, they cleaned out her house. My sister sent me all these letters that Mom had written but never mailed to me. When I read them, as a sixty-year-old, I saw she was terrified of what could happen to me. I was her oldest, and she didn't know what to do to keep me from falling apart. She didn't mention addiction in these notes. She called it exhaustion: "You need to just rest." My mother chased a good night's sleep her entire life and now I do the same.

Drinking brought me back to myself. It was the thing that tied me back to my spirit. After that first night of throwing up, the worry lifted for the first time in my life. Drinking, and donning Bonne Bell lip gloss and making out with boys, rubbed away the worry like soda water on a wine stain.

No elbow grease needed.

The next weekend, I walked downtown and paid some older boys to get me a bottle of rum from the LCBO. By the end of the summer, I had been hospitalized for alcohol poisoning.

My mother picked me up the morning after my stomach had been pumped. "Ever since you fell off that bike, you think everything is a joke," she said. "Well, everything is not a joke."

DOES YOUR FAMILY FIND YOU STRANGE?

Two years after I told mom I left Church, I was standing in front of the receptionist in the shrink's office wearing huge gold-rimmed sunglasses—not because I was worried that people would recognize me (I only knew a handful of people in Saskatchewan), but because I had a nervous tic in my left eye that made me look like I was winking at people.

I was the first to leave home. All my cousins were headed out west to work in the oil fields, but my first step toward independence flung me only half an hour away at the community college in Belleville. In my second year, I began working at the local radio station as a disc jockey and subbing in the copy department. Even as a kid I had been thinking up ad campaigns and sending them out to big companies. At the time, there was an ad on TV for Kellogg's Raisin Bran boasting about how there were two scoops of raisins in every box. I wrote a commercial from one of the bran flakes' point of view. Bradley the Bran Flake, a bran flake who wore glasses and a bow tie, trundled into Mr. Kellogg's office and complained that the raisins were getting all the attention which wasn't fair since, "All the bran flakes were crispy even in milk." I found a raisin in my mom's baking items and spent hours studying its shape and drawing raisins until my eyes were bleary. Then I sent it to Kellogg's and got a very nice letter back commending my imagination.

Another ad campaign I created as a teenager was for the Holiday Inn, where the Virgin Mary and Joseph came with their new baby and the hotel concierge gets them a great room, then turns to the camera and says, "There is always room at the Inn." The Holiday Inn wrote me a very indignant letter, saying my ideas would likely offend their religious clientele.

After a couple of years at the Belleville radio station, I moved to Regina to write copy for a country music station and learned more than anyone needs to know about noxious weeds and bull insemination. A few months in, I got another job writing ad campaigns for the NDP. But even the great money the socialists paid couldn't keep away the darkness that had begun to descend again. I thought I was covering it quite well until my boss came into my office, shut the door behind her and whispered that she thought I might be depressed.

"Nothing to be ashamed of, Deb. I too have struggled with the black dog." Her hair was blond and she had long, red nails she tapped on my desk. Her skin was so pale I worried the fluorescent lights might give her sunstroke.

The word *depressed* was not in the mainstream vernacular in the late '70s. Words for your feelings had not yet come into vogue. If you were sad, you had "a case of the blues" or were "suffering from nerve trouble." Nerve trouble was any behaviour that people in your community deemed odd. That covered a wide range of symptoms, from something as simple as serving carrot cake instead of pie to trying to shoot your family in an alcohol-fuelled blackout.

When my boss mentioned the word *depression*, I wanted to joke it off. *Of course I'm depressed. I'm writing pithy slogans for the NDP. I listen to socialist civil servants argue for hours over where to place an* a *or a* the. *The Bible didn't have that many rewrites.*

I tried to convince myself my bleak mood was only homesickness. I was a thousand miles from home, in a place so flat the wide-open spaces caused me to hyperventilate. I was an Ontario girl and needed hills and trees to feel secure. Natives of the province would try to cheer me up by driving me out to Fort Qu'Appelle to show off their only mountain. Sheer hyperbole. It was a mere bump, the one spot where God created a bit of cleavage across Saskatchewan's flat chest.

Winter was endless. In this place, surviving one freezing winter after another was a bragging right. "It's a dry cold," they'd say, as if that made it better. Any temperature that is measured by how long you would survive if you fell into a snowbank is cold. I found this out the night I got loaded after work and passed out in a snowbank behind the radio station. The weatherman saw me, dragged me inside, lectured me on wind chill and then slept with me to warm me up.

After the snowbank incident, I quit drinking for a while, which took me back to weeks of insomnia like I had experienced in high school. I would pass the wee hours of the morning reading a book about Ukrainian mail-order brides. Besides being married off to some man they had never met before, they had come from Ukraine to end up in this cold, flat place, as bad or worse than the place they had just left. At four in the morning, I'd lie awake wondering which part was worse: being stuck in this land of infinite cold or having sex with a man you didn't know? *Go to sleep, Deb. Count your lucky stars that you're not a mail-order bride.*

Of course, I *wasn't* stuck in Regina. I could've easily got on a plane and flown home. But I had convinced myself I couldn't go back with my tail between my legs, despite the fact my parents and friends couldn't care less. For them, there was no tail. No legs. My friends missed me, and my parents wondered what I was doing out here in the first place.

I didn't know anything about mental health issues. I thought I felt this way because I wasn't a good person. I began worrying that an evil force would overtake me. *Again.* I read the *Catholic Register* magazine my mother mailed to me every month, not for its unbiased journalistic style, but as a form of protection. Despite my big proclamation of not being Catholic, I went back to Sunday Mass, then committed to a second Mass on the first Friday of the month. None of it helped the sinking feeling. So I tried harder and, before I knew it, I was going to church four or five times a week, often during my lunch hour. While others were eating tuna sandwiches in a food court somewhere, I was sneaking off to genuflect and spritz myself with holy water.

The insomnia and dread didn't subside at all, so I upped the ante by performing charitable acts for an old lady called Eva. Or maybe she was called Ava. Or Ada. I can't remember her name, but she sat a few pews ahead of me at church, her back bent into a question mark, whispering her way around the glass beads the way Grandma used to do. One day, I cornered her after Mass and asked if she'd like to go for coffee.

Soon after, I began to visit her after church on Sundays, and in her one-room flat she served me pickled herring with sour cream, which made me gag. I ate jars of the stuff, hoping the herring might get me holy enough to get some sleep. I didn't like EvaAvaAda. She was a hoarder and her apartment smelled of urine, and after an hour of her long, sad stories about her homeland Poland and how the Nazis occupied Warsaw, I'd leave more depressed than ever. I'd smile and try to look interested, nodding and saying yes in all the right places, but I kept bursting into tears. I hoped EvaAvaAda would think my tears were because of her terrible trials, but one day as I sat there pouring out my crocodile tears, she looked up at me and said, "You are too sad. You are too, too sad." When a survivor of the Warsaw Uprising tells you that you are "too, too sad," you know there's something too, too wrong.

All this praying and crying led me to my doctor, which led me to a shrink in the same day. The medical establishment is the only place where you get nervous when you get excellent service. When I checked in for my appointment, the nurse gave me tons of forms—endless pages of multiple-choice questions.

"Fill out these papers and the doctor will assess you."

I had to poke holes in the paper to choose the answer to the yes or no questions.

"1. Do you have suicidal thoughts?" I drove a hole in the "yes" column. I never thought of suicide but felt they wouldn't take me seriously if I hadn't.

"2. Do you want to harm others?" "No." I did want to harm others, but I wasn't going to tell them that.

"3. Do you lie?" Refer to questions 1 and 2.

My favourite question of the bunch:

"5. Does your family find you strange?" Of course they do! That's why I am in Regina trying to get away from them. A much smarter question would have been, "Do you find your family strange?" I would've aced that question. But there is no essay portion when you are getting a mental health assessment.

I didn't know what answers they wanted to hear. *Which ones will make me look sane enough to stay out of the hospital, but crazy enough to get some help?* I began randomly poking as many holes in the form as I could. There were so many holes in my test papers, they looked like they had been in the crossfire of a Mafia hitman. When I walked into the psychiatrist's office, he sat at his desk and waved the test sheets. *Don't wink at the shrink*, I willed myself behind my gold-rimmed sunglasses.

He looked over his spectacles (shrinks wear spectacles, not glasses): "Well, it would appear you are a sociopathic paranoid with schizophrenic tendencies." No wonder I couldn't sleep. "Has this kind of insomnia ever happened before?"

"Yes, when I was seventeen. I was afraid to close my eyes."

"Why?"

"You know, because if I went to sleep, I feared Satan might take over my soul."

"Satan?"

"He didn't actually do it and that is because I said the rosary, and I wore extra underpants."

"Excuse me. What? Underpants? You thought that extra pairs of underpants could stop Satan?"

"No, you can't stop Satan with extra underpants." *Who is this guy? Does he not know anything at all about the Lord of the Underworld?*

"Was there a man in your life who may have crawled into your bed? A man who might have wanted to hurt you?"

"No. No. There was no man near my underpants. Listen, it's not like that. I am talking about the real Devil here, you know. Have you ever seen the movie *The Exorcist*?"

"You watched this *Exorcist* movie, and now you are afraid someone will crawl into your underpants?" The psychiatrist was shaking his head and furiously taking notes. "And did you ever get help back then?"

"Help? No. I just went to church. I confessed to a priest, and he said ..."

"What did he say?"

"He said despair was a sin."

"Good grief. Despair is not a sin." The shrink's face softened, and he smiled as if he felt sorry for me. "It's going to be okay. You come back here next Wednesday and we will talk. Oh, and you will need this." He tore a sheet off his prescription pad and handed it to me. I was sure it was for drugs. It was not. *Why do doctors never give me any drugs? Do they take one look at me and think drugs would be redundant?* Written on the paper were two words: "Father Tom."

"You're sending me to a priest?"

"Yes. Tom works at the university with young people like you who have, um, spiritual issues."

"Spiritual issues?"

"It appears you're extremely Catholic."

"I am not Catholic. I quit being Catholic a few years back."

"Oh? Then why are you going to church every day?" One of my eyes began twitching, and I was now winking at him like crazy under my glasses. He smiled. "It's going to be okay. Father Tom will help." I left the office confused. Why would someone call you extremely Catholic then send you to a priest? Maybe it's like getting a flu shot. If you inject more of the virus into the body, it will create immunity against the disease.

GOD'S A HARD NUT TO CRACK

Father Tom was a "Don't-call-me-Father-call-me-Tommy" kind of priest with coyote-blue eyes. I fell in love with him at first glance. I was sure he would fall in love with me and maybe leave the priesthood. Once I stopped crying.

"Dr. Matthews said you're having a wee crisis of faith?" Crisis was an understatement. I hadn't slept in weeks and I was now wearing three pairs of granny panties to bed.

"Listen, Father, let's cut to the chase. I want to know one thing and one thing only: Is there evil in the world? Yes, or no?"

"Yes, evil exists in the world."

What a terrible answer.

"Really?" I asked, furious that he couldn't come up with something a little more comforting.

He smiled. "I believe there is also good in the world. Good always trumps evil."

"Yes, but what if good can't trump evil? What if in the rock-paper-scissors game of life, evil is as powerful as good?"

"Well, evil can trump good if we don't actively campaign against it. Evil happens when good people do nothing. That is why we must take the right actions."

"Do you think Satan can come in the middle of the night and take over my soul?"

"That's not how Satan works. He doesn't crawl into your soul in the middle of the night. It's what we do and how we act that constitutes good or evil." I don't know how he knew these things, but I suppose there was a manual he had read while in the seminary. A manual that outlined Satan's job description and work hours.

"Tell me about your upbringing," he continued.

"Well, we had six kids and ..."

"And what about your dad?"

"My dad was Protestant. He worked like the devil."

"He took the Protestant work ethic to heart?"

My dad worked till it hurt. I remember he'd come home exhausted at ten o'clock at night, sometimes with body parts missing. Black eyes. Twisted knees. One time he had a huge chunk of skin gone from his elbow and when we asked him what had happened, he looked at it and said, "Damn it. I wondered where that bleeding was coming from."

"Dad was Protestant. Irish. He was orange Irish. Mom was Catholic. She was green Irish, which on a paint pallet makes a bloody mess. And once they got engaged, he converted to Catholicism and never ate a piece of meat on a Friday ever again. Because Mom would have crucified him."

"Crucified him?"

This was a forty-five-minute session, so I didn't have time to go into all the crucifixion threats, so I changed direction. "We prayed a lot. We said the rosary nearly every night of our lives."

"Every night? Wow." Father Tom asked.

"Well, Monday to Friday. Sometimes, I would answer the phone after these prayer sessions with 'Hail Mary full of grace,' rather than hello."

Father Tom laughed out loud. He found the whole thing funny. He downright guffawed when I told him Mom made us say a

41

thousand Hail Marys on Good Friday. "We cleaned and prayed at the same time. Whenever she walked by me sweeping, I'd make the same hissing sound I had heard my Grandma Brady make when she said her prayers—whispering like a fly stuck in a window. Mom thought I was praying, but for me it was like I was beating her at her own game."

"A thousand Hail Marys? Where did she come up with that number?"

Didn't he know? Wasn't that the recommended dosage?

I went on to tell him how I was dragged from one shrine to another to cure my psoriasis. "I hoped God would heal me. Year after year, I prayed that my dead skin would be removed and left on the altar alongside the canes and wooden legs. But what if it got vacuumed up?"

"You have psoriasis? Have you ever tried giving up drinking milk?"

I gave up milk, soaked my skin with jars of Vaseline, wore two pairs of beige leotards so flakes wouldn't seep through. "I have tried everything, okay, Tom?" I paused. "Is there something wrong with me?"

Father Tom got quiet and gently said, "I don't think so, but I do think maybe religion doesn't need to be this hard."

What was he talking about? Of course it needs to be this hard. What right does this hippie guy have to tell me religion is easy?

"God makes it easy for those that seek," Father Tom told me.

Oh, really? He was obviously pushing the party line, but how could anyone ever say seeking God was easy?

"Maybe if you came here for a few weeks, you'd get some sleep."

The promise of sleep sealed the deal. I dumped EvaAvaAda and began seeing Father Tom once a week. I saw the shrink as well. He gave me a book called *Hope and Help for Your Nerves* by Claire Weekes, which described how my brain worked and how anxiety got triggered. Until then, I thought my thoughts were dangerous—something to be overcome or avoided altogether.

I have read many self-help books in my life, and I can tell you, if you glean one nugget from two hundred pages, you're lucky. The author of this book suggested the mantra "Breathe. Float. Let Time Pass," and I still use those words to calm my nerves.

Dr. Matthews handled my mind, and Father Tom handled my spiritual questioning. I started taking the bus out to the university Mass every Saturday evening. Tommy, as he now insisted I call him, would stand up at the front of the room, the mostly female crowd hanging off every word he said. When he brought out his guitar after the homily, we all went weak in the knees. Most priests sang "Make Me a Channel of Your Peace" as a dirge; he turned it into something akin to Glen Campbell's "Rhinestone Cowboy." One week he sang "It's Good News Week," the same song I sang during my Christmas concerts. No wonder we had connected on a heart level. *We were soulmates.* Sometimes he went rogue and played "(I Can't Get No) Satisfaction," which seemed like an apt anthem for an unmarried man. I had a crush. Bigtime.

By this point in time, the gospel had been translated into everyday language, and Tommy peppered his sermons with modern-day vernacular. "If Jesus were here, would he be a guy you'd hang out with? Would you go out to a movie with him? I mean, he's just a guy, isn't he? A guy who had a human experience just like us. Hanging out with our Lord, could you dig it?" Some phrases cause involuntary retching in me, and "Can you dig it?" is one of them, but Tommy was revolutionizing my life, so I overlooked his hippie verbiage.

One Sunday morning, he handed out walnuts to all the parishioners and then held one up between his thumb and pointer finger. He had very tiny hands with clean, clipped fingernails. He said,

"God's love is like this walnut. It may be a hard nut to crack, but inside it's rich and meaty."

I went home and immediately put that walnut on my bedside table. In the wee hours before dawn, I entertained myself by imagining how rich and meaty God's love would be if I cracked open the nut. On the way out to our next weekly session, I came up with many funny nut analogies to impress Tommy, but he didn't care. He just wanted to talk about my insane mother. "I want you to know: she is not God."

Really? Did anyone tell her that?

Later in my life, I did think Tommy was on to something. He explained that when we are children, our parents seem like gods to us. They have all the power over every part of our day. What we do and think.

"Well, tell me again," said Tommy, "why did your mother want to crucify you?"

"I don't know. It's just something she said when she was frustrated."

"Your mom is some piece of work," he said, tying his hair into a ponytail.

I loved bitching about my mother more than anyone else did, but being in cahoots with Tommy was starting to make me feel nauseous.

"Listen, I don't want to talk about my mom anymore." Tommy's tone annoyed me. What right did he have to diagnose her as odd? That was my job. *I didn't come here to find more ways to hate her, Tommy. I am already doing a very good job of that on my own.* Besides, he'd never met my mother. He didn't have kids, so he didn't know what stress she was under. Dad worked all the time, morning to night, and she never got a break from us. In fact, weren't guys like Tommy part of the problem? She had been brainwashed into thinking she had to have all those kids.

44

Even though I was complaining about how I was raised, I still wanted to find a way to understand my mother. To love her like I had as a child. When I was little, I thought the sun rose and set on my mother. I had always wanted to please her. I was her best helper. I performed elaborate plays at the end of her bed that made her laugh. I wrote her encouraging letters listing in point form what she was doing right and made cards with macaroni glued to the front. Cards that told her she was not just a good mother but the best mother in the entire world.

That was the beginning of the end for Tommy and me. The next week I cancelled our private session. I said I had a cold. Or was it my appendix? I don't know. I was always lying about one illness or another back then. On the following Saturday, I decided that it was ridiculous taking the bus out to the university for a Mass that took too long. *I am only twenty-two. Why am I spending my time worrying about the workings of the universe?* Mom might not be God, but neither was Tommy. *How dare he make me have a crush on him.* He was an unmarried man who thought he was morally superior to the rest of us.

With Saturday nights free, I called EvaAvaAda to see if she had received a new shipment of Śledzie marynowane or Polish herring, but when she heard it was me, she said she was too busy to talk. "Sorry, Deb. I have friends over." *Really, EvaAvaAda?* I was sick of EvaAvaAda and my pious posing. I called a friend from work who invited me to tag along to the Oktoberfest celebrations. Maybe drinking German beer and doing slap-the-knee Schuhplattler dancing would help raise the serotonin. At the end of the evening, all the young women lined up, linked arms and competed to see who could kick their legs the highest. I made it to runner-up. But in the final round, I was disqualified when I fell backward—ass over teakettle—landing on my wrist. The night ended with me in an emergency room, screaming at the doctors,

45

"You better not cast my arm because I need it to write propaganda for the socialist government!" They gave me a brace for my wrist and a Valium to shut me up. The security guard from Oktoberfest, who had accompanied me to the hospital, offered to drive me back to my apartment. As I stumbled out of his car, I purred, "Call me sometime." Then I added one more amuse-bouche for good measure: "I will write you your very own commercial."

The next morning, as he grabbed his watch off the night table, he saw my walnut sitting there. "What are you doing with a nut beside your bed?" *What am I doing with a nut in my bed?*

I batted my eyes and said in a sultry voice, "The walnut represents the meaty, rich love of God." He turned to me and said, "What if you crack it open and it is rotten inside?" Then he stood up, strapped his walkie-talkie around his waist like a six shooter, and swaggered out.

This kind of scene happened again and again for the next ten years: The struggle between Good Deb and Bad Deb. The pious, devout child who tried to help, and the rebellious teenager who'd light her head on fire just to see what smoke smelled like.

ALCHEMY

Both **Father Tom** and the shrink independently declared that with my overactive imagination, I would make a great con artist or a great writer, so naturally I decided to move to Toronto to become an actor.

Today, young people are encouraged to be creative, but in our family, creativity was considered almost a mental illness. "She's a bit of an 'artsy one,'" they said with air quotes.

There is a picture of me in a ballet performance at five years of age. We are wearing checkered aprons and holding brooms for some reason. Perhaps the ballet was about cleaning or curling? All the girls have their right foot in front of their left. Both my feet are splayed out like I am giving birth to a bowling ball. The other girls' heads are facing left, but mine is looking to the right like I am an explorer looking to discover foreign lands. "You were up there staring off into space," my mother said, "like you were having a chat with the fairies." No matter my future successes, this picture was often pulled out as evidence of being a dreamer.

Doing a ballet class as a child was one thing, but choosing to stand out as a career was quite another. I took acting classes at night and, to make ends meet, I served up pre-game grub at

Smoky's, the restaurant across from the Maple Leaf Gardens. Leafs fans and concertgoers were great tippers so I raked in the dough but everything I was doing was based on blind hope that this comedy thing was going to work out.

My other Joe job was being hired as a mail sorter at an aluminum company in the west end of Toronto. My job title was Mail Girl. The mail girl shredded documents in the back room, practiced monologues from classic plays, did grocery shopping and made lunch for the male executives, Scott and Bill, and delivered their hotlunches at noon on the dot. Apparently, feminism had bypassed this organization all together. I did comedy bits for them, and one day, after performing my daily set, Bill said that he and Scott wanted to treat me to a show at the Second City. The Second City originated in Chicago, and since New York was the first city Chicago was the second. After that one show—watching the performers do mouth karate, zigging and zagging, weaving ideas into their skits no matter what the audience threw at them—I was hooked.

"You're as funny as they are. Forget about being a serious actress and do that," Bill or Scott said.

I knew I could make people laugh. But as a career choice? Being funny wasn't encouraged the way other talents were. In school, if you sang, you got sent to the music teacher; if you lifted something up over your head, you got sent to the gym. But if you were funny, you got sent to the principal's office.

I was never the class clown because I was never in class. I was the one who mocked the class clown, out in the smoking area while bumming cigarettes. I majored in euchre and making out with a hockey player or two. And by my senior year Mom couldn't tell my grades from my days missed.

But after that night at Second City, I saw this is what I was meant to do. As a child, every room in the house had been my stage. I'd spend hours performing commercials in front of the bathroom mirror, washing half of my head with ordinary shampoo and half of it with suds-free Breck.

All those hours, pretending I was a famous movie star who was on Johnny Carson, and at night I'd nudge my sister awake and tell her to interview me. I even had the questions written out for her.

"Debbie, what do you attribute your success to?"

"Well, I think it was a lot of hard work and the love of Jesus Christ." I had heard Oscar winners thank Jesus.

I was in the variety night in high school and wrote skits and got "booked" to write comedic turns for Grandma Kimmett's Women's Institute.

The Women's Institute was an organization that encouraged rural women to come together to challenge themselves mentally and become activists in the community. My grandma was a lifetime member who cooked hundreds of dinners for them at the Napanee Fair, standing in that hot booth for three days straight serving up hot turkey dinners. Grandma loved everything I did and wanted to show me off. When she introduced me, she instructed the women of the Empey Hill W.I. on how to behave when I performed. Grandma dropped out of school when she was a girl, and she never lost her slow hillbilly twang. "My granddaughter Debi Kimmett is on the program tonight, ladies. This girl could make a dog laugh. So just remember she is starting out and she doesn't know nuthin'." Despite Grandma's strong-arming, and no matter how funny I was, there was always some helmet-headed, slack-jawed woman who'd come up to me after and say, "Well ain't that different, Debi."

So, I harkened destiny's call, and took Bill and Scott's advice and signed up for improvisation classes at Second City. From that first class, I felt like my messy brain had finally found a place to stretch out and relax. I could say anything off the top of my head, and instead of demanding literal truth, the classes encouraged me to build and exaggerate ideas to get a laugh. Exaggeration got me into trouble everywhere else in my life, but here it was a requirement. Mom had gone to normal school to be a teacher when she was barely seventeen. In fact, that's how she met my dad: he dropped off his brothers to the one-room school she was teaching in. Motherhood may have curtailed that career, until much later in life, but teaching was in her bones. She was on top of every error—she'd even spell-check my Mother's Day cards. Doing things the right way was the enemy of improv. Mistakes were where the magic was.

After six weeks of taking classes, I auditioned and got hired for the Second City touring company and I had found my tribe. My family didn't know what to make of it. They were great storytellers. Most of my relatives could also tell a story that would make a dog laugh, but they never thought that a person could make a living from doing it. Mom's reaction to me being hired was that I better not put her in one of my shows. (I put her in every single one of my shows.)

When I told Dad I was going to be a comic, we were at the bus station and, as he handed me my suitcase, I said, "I'm going to be a comic."

He climbed back in his van and placed his elbow on the window and said, "Well, you've picked a helluva row to hoe. One day you'll want people to take you seriously, and they won't." Then he cleaned out his ear with a nail and drove off.

When I told Grandma Kimmett the news, she opined, "Why couldn't you get a part in *General Hospital*? That way, I could see you every day."

To my brother Kevin, my artistic choice made no economic sense. "Acting is like going to the track. Your horse wins just enough to keep you hooked."

He wasn't wrong about that. Dad wasn't wrong either. I had picked a helluva row to hoe. As much as it looked like you could say anything you wanted, improvisation was a demanding art form. There was a certain kind of math to it: two set-up lines and the blow. The blow is the punchline. But three set-up lines and the blow won't work. You will always get a laugh at an odd number, but never an even one. Though I found math difficult in high school, I loved these kinds of calculations. Performing live was exhilarating and unpredictable. One night the audience was fantastic, and the next, they were too drunk and obnoxious to know where they were. My performing skills were equally erratic. One night, I was hilarious; the next night, I smelled up the place. When a scene began to nosedive, I didn't have enough experience to course correct.

My mother's incessant criticism of me had been bootcamp for the director, named Jeff. He had been the carpenter at The Second City, and they liked him so much they promoted him to director. Appropriate, because his notes were like a two-by-four to the head. He kept hammering home how untalented we were. Most of the cast nodded their heads, then when he left they did what they wanted, but not me. I had a meltdown after nearly every show. One of my fellow cast members said he had seen me cry more in nine months than he'd seen his wife cry in nine years. Despite all that weeping, I got promoted to Mainstage Second City in Toronto.

I worked with the brilliant director Del Close, a wild man hired from Second City Chicago. Del's antics were legendary in improv circles. He had quit drinking but replaced it with pot and any other drug he could inhale. There was a bar at the back of the theatre, and he'd often snort nitrous oxide from the whipped cream canisters. You knew Del had helped himself to a hit when one of the waiters would yell out, "Jesus, Del! Now how am I supposed to make a Spanish coffee?"

Del was as sexist as any other man of the time, making outrageous statements about the female species. But that's the way it was everywhere. Sexism was built into the comedy world, and women endured it. It was the only way to get to do what we loved. It's not that we didn't notice it, and we stood up for ourselves, but you could be as feminist as it gets and it did no good. These were the days before women were considered funny.

At Second City, we were outnumbered two women to four men (a number that continued until the 2000s when the ratio switched to three women to four men), so the men in our troupe decided what would and wouldn't work. Not because they were funnier than us but because they had the more significant vote. No matter how hard we developed our voice and followed the rules, the men were always deferred to. Male comics, by nature, are a clowder of feral cats. You can't rein them in. But when it came to deciding what was deemed funny, they were pack animals. If a man suggested an idea and other men laughed at it, they were golden—The End.

As women, we had to contour ourselves to fit in. We talked dirty, tried to out-funny them, then put them in their place by calling them sexist (then sleeping with them, stalking them and making them cookies). All our attempts made no difference. If we didn't come up with ideas the men found funny, we were vetoed. If we accommodated them too much, we were considered weak. *A pussy.* Pussy: a body part that they couldn't get enough of off stage, but in this setting was considered a put-down. We fought not to play the foil or "straight woman," but it was a delicate balance. If we were too angry on stage, the audience thought we were being bitches. It took years for me to understand that if you are a funny woman, people will always tell you what you can and can't say. If I could go back to that time and talk to my younger self, I would say to her: "Relax. There is no way to make everyone happy. So you might as well do what you want."

Del's sexism was no worse than anyone else's. At least he was an intelligent sexist with a brain unfettered by convention. A man in black with fingernails to match. Not polish, but dirt. His hair was never combed. Del hung out in the right side of his brain—before I met him, I didn't even know I had two sides to my brain—and invited us to sit with him. He would take a flicker of an idea—one of our afterthoughts we'd race past—and show us how to beat it out. Beat out means to tease out, imbuing something with elevation and exaggeration and making it funny. He taught me improv was like walking a tightrope—but when you fell off there was another tightrope waiting for you to land on.

Improv has an odd alchemy. The chemistry of you and your scene partner, combined with the audience's energy, created a third substance. Some nights it was gold, and others, we were tin men peddling scrap metal. On stage and off stage were two different worlds. On stage, I was immersed in another world, exchanging energy with the cast and the audience. When it worked, you were a goddess. You touched the cloak of Bacchus, and the divine let you in on the secrets of the universe. Making people laugh is an elixir like no other. You could be sick as a dog backstage, running a fever of 102, but on stage, you transcended all limitations of the body. The illness got put on the shelf for the length of the show, but the moment you stepped off stage, you could no longer fly. Like Icarus you fell into the ocean, a mere mortal with broken bones and a fever.

When audience members would come backstage and tell me things that they found funny, there was a part of me that was surprised that they had seen me. *Oh, you saw me do that.* I was like a kid standing behind a tree, thinking I was invisible. It was all-consuming when I was performing. It was the only time in my life when other people's opinions were not stuck to me.

When my parents came to see me, I would look out from the backstage curtain before the show and see them in the audience. Dad often would enlist a bunch of his friends to make the two-and-a-half-hour trek, take them out for supper and bring them to my show. I can still see him laughing at me on stage while simultaneously looking around to see who in the audience was laughing too. If he did make eye contact with a fellow audience member, he would point to the stage and say, "That's my girl." But after the show, he'd act like I'd not performed at all. After seeing him laugh so hard, I'd come out expecting a compliment, but he'd nod his head and ask,

"So, what have you been up to, Debbie?"

Performing, Dad! Didn't you see me up there, performing?

Instead, I'd say, "Nothing, Dad. How about you?"

My mother, on the other hand, sat in the audience, arms crossed, head down like she was about to hear a guilty verdict from a jury, but by the end of the show her cheeks were wet with laughter. She could never offer any praise, though. Once, when she saw me backstage, the first thing she said was that the sleeves in my jacket were too short. "For God's sake, take that off so I can let the hem down on those sleeves. You look like a ragamuffin."

Mom commented on how well everybody's clothes fit. Their jackets, their buttons, but especially their pants. She could take one look at your ass and tell you what size pants you needed. I hated her for it, but I never had to return a pair of slacks. This talent had been awakened when she had taken a pants-making course that the Women's Institute offered, and after that, she couldn't stop looking at people's crotches. "If the crotch smiles, the pants are too tight. If the crotch frowns, the pants are too loose." Years later, when I took her to see *Mamma Mia!*, she couldn't focus on the performance because Louise Pitre's crotch smiled at her all through "Dancing Queen."

Back then, I acted the way many twenty-somethings do when their mothers don't respond perfectly to their lives: "Why do you have to wreck everything in my life?" I think my relationship with my parents would've been perfect if I had just stayed on stage and they had stayed in the audience, and we had never had to deal with each other for the rest of our lives.

We had eight shows a week and each audience had its own personality. Producers from places like *Saturday Night Live* would be looking for future stars, and there was a corner in the back where the understudies and the up and coming stood wanting our jobs. Vultures' Corner. And I was up there "yes-anding" as fast as I could, trying to hit perfection.

But improvisation is not for perfectionists. It's all about making mistakes and getting up and trying again. On stage, the improv style of theatre suited me, but inside myself, that weird little girl was trying to get it right. But there was no time to perfect anything. There was another show the next night, and you had to get back up there and try to become a goddess again. It was hard work to clear away the ego enough to access that kind of energy every night. Sometimes you were brilliant. More nights than not the muse seemed to be screening your calls.

There is an intimacy within the members of an improv cast because you all know what it is like to risk failure every night. After the show, we'd hang out and kibitz for a while, but before long, I would leave. I needed to be alone to piece myself back together again. I needed to find a dark place where I could be invisible, with no eyes on me. It was the way I came back to myself. I'd frequent a booze can called Richard and Patty's on Queen West. An illegal after-hours club with an open room above a bank at Queen and Spadina. A place called Scotty's had been downstairs years before, but someone had been shot there, and they hadn't reopened. Someone having been shot just two floors down was part of the appeal of Richard and Patty's.

The doors opened at midnight, and it was frequented by musicians and theatre folks wearing Mary Quant mascara, dressed in black garb and gunner boots. I wore dresses from the vintage shops in Kensington. Some nights I worked the bar, but often

I was the party starter who chatted people up and got them in the mood for fun. I'd stand in the middle of the floor and dance solo. There was a parachute hanging from the ceiling with twinkly white Christmas lights. Techno music pumped, and eventually Georgie Purple, one of the male strippers from Zanzibar, would slide across the hardwood floor covered in dancing crystals, doing the Lido Hustle. Georgie preened in front of the mirror—like Narcissus, clocking his head movements when he twirled around.

The ghouls would go home at 5 a.m., at the first sign of dawn. Vampires hate the light. And the magic would disappear, and we'd clean up, and after Patty and Richard and I would go for breakfast at a place I think was called Barney's Diner. Then I'd go home and do *20 Minute Workout*—an exercise show that aired twice daily on the local station, CityTV. *You need to take care of your body.*

I'd sleep away the day, then I'd go to rehearsal in the afternoon and perform again at night and drink all night and do it all over again.

If you disassociate from your body, it's called trauma. If you disassociate and get paid for it, it's called a comedy career.

I was obsessed with comedy and with men. Specifically with a man called Bill the Postman. He was a union buster for Canada Post and about ten years my senior. We met after a show one night, and when he said he wanted a casual relationship, I said I wanted a committed one. We got together the way many lovers do, hoping one of us would change our minds. We broke up six times in about as many months. It only made sense we would try to get back together on New Year's Eve, a night that only Valentine's Day surpasses for expectations of a good time.

That afternoon, I went back to Kensington Market and pur-
chased a 1940s grey gown with matching gloves that went up to my
elbow. When Bill showed up two hours late in ripped jeans (an out-
fit that did not match my high hopes), I was a few martinis in. We
sat at the kitchen table; we dissected our relationship over some
vodka and crudités. Celery and carrots with onion dip. When we
hit our usual impasse, I asked where we were going for dinner. A
man so commitment-phobic was above making reservations. We
walked up and down Bloor Street until we finally got into a local
burger joint where we fought and drank and fought some more. It
was in this state that we hit the New Year's Eve party at Theatre
Passe Muraille. It was a party with the who's who of the theatre.
The place was teeming with playwrights and actors. Drinks were
flowing in red plastic cups, and the floor was sticky with beer. Bill
went off to a room somewhere to get high.

I hated drugs. I had read *Go Ask Alice* and got scared I'd end
up like her. Instead, I chugged vodka from up on my high horse.

In the main theatre was a stripper named Spiderman, whom
I'd met at Patty and Richard's, who was winding himself around
black nets hanging from the ceiling. Turning himself in and out of
black cords, he worked the crowd into a frenzy. I was catcalling
with everyone else when Bill returned bleary-eyed. Looking at
his baked smile made me furious. We got into it. An epic "Screw
you!" "No, screw you!" screaming match, ending with me attempt-
ing to kick him in the ass—but as I was about to make contact, he
grabbed my leg and the heel of my shoe snapped off. I hobbled
off alone onto Queen Street West, which was teeming with New
Year's Eve revellers.

I was *that* girl you see walking down a street late at night.
That girl with mascara dripping down her cheek to her cleavage,
oozing tragedy. Head held high because at the time pathetic was
its own badge of honour.

Midnight hit. Fireworks were popping off from a distance at Harbourfront. People spilled from the bars singing "Auld Lang Syne" and swinging their noisemakers. Strangers offered kisses. A cab driver pulled up and drove alongside me.

"Smile, darling, it can't be that bad."

I turned to him and pouted. "I got nobody to kiss." *What a catch I was.*

"I'll kiss you," he said as he put the car in park, and I climbed in.

After we finished making out, I hobbled down the street with my shoe heel in hand, one leg two inches shorter than the other. When I got to my house, I saw Bill's car parked there. He hadn't wanted to drive after he'd been drinking. I picked up a mallet. Our landlord had been renovating and had left it on my verandah. If he was going to mess me up, I would hit him where it hurt most: his 1972 Volvo.

I hoisted the giant hammer above my head, and as I went to lower it, Kenny, my roommate, swept in and grabbed it from me. "No, Deb! No. Don't." I tried to grab it again, but he scooped me up into his arms and flipped me over his shoulder. Kenny danced for City Ballet. He had good core strength. As I hung over him, I reached over and pulled off Bill's driver's side windshield wiper with my free hand. "Jesus. You're like kerosene. You are flammable." Kenny held tight as I kicked and screamed for him to let me go; he did an allegro walk back to the house.

He and a man that he had picked up in the baths poured me several shots of Drambuie until I melted into the couch. I woke up sometime the next afternoon, head pounding. Kenny was still sawing logs in the chair next to me. His drive-by lover had left sometime in the night. When I looked out the window, I saw Bill wiping the snow off his car. I had to tell him about the windshield wiper. I opened the front door and stood in the doorway in my silk pajamas. With my hair seductively hanging over one eye, I purred, "Come inside, babe! We need to talk."

And he said what every girl wants to hear at that moment, "Get away from me, you insane bitch."

If that was the way he was going to act, then I wasn't going to admit to anything. I watched him drive off, one hand on the steering wheel and the other wiping the falling snow off his windshield.

This was how 1981 began. The year Diana and Charles would get engaged. A couple of years before AIDS became an epidemic. And the year a Buddhist named Marie Hopps taught me how to meditate.

LET GO
OF THE
BOUNCING BALL

The first time I stumbled into Marie Hopps's plant-filled apartment, I resembled a feral cat, hair matted, and shaking from a few nights on a prowl. She and I had met when I was in the Second City touring company, and she'd offered to teach me how to act.

At least forty years my senior, Marie, British, had white hair tied back in a bun. She'd make me tea and then try to look interested while I butchered the greats. Shakespeare, Shaw and Beckett, I destroyed them all. Eventually, the formal lessons fell away, and she listened to my endless dating problems. Today she'd be called a life coach, but to me, she was the woman who mothered me.

She gave me unconditional love. I would babble for an hour about some injustice the man of the day had committed. There was no shortage of stories, for Bill was gone and I had entered my musical phase: dating musicians of all stripes and varying degrees of talent, who often had a huge head start on me with their addictions. A drummer who once played with the Alice Cooper band drove me out of my mind for about three years. I was trying to convince him to pay as much attention to me as he did to cocaine.

Many nights after the show at Second City, I'd go searching for him in bars all over Toronto. Then I was called persistent. Today there would be a restraining order. These were the days before the internet, so you couldn't text or put a tracking app on your phone. In my day, lovers had to roll themselves off their futon, get dressed and call a cab *with a rotary phone* to torture each other.

When I did manage to track him down at the Jarvis House, or some dive bar on Queen West, he'd be passed out in the back at a table covered in a towel, which would soak up the spilled beer. I'd poke him awake and he'd give me a look that said, "God, woman, I was hoping I'd finally lost you." The drummer, like me, wanted to sit in the dark alone. Instead, he'd get a lecture and a drink thrown in his face and, for a dramatic finish, a slammed door. "I don't care if you don't want to get together. Just phone me and let me know you are okay. That's all I want." I'd say the same line to every man I dated. What a crock. That's not all I wanted at all. That's not what any stalker wants. I wanted him to change.

The morning after hunting down the drummer, I'd be remorseful, hoping that he had been in a blackout the night before and we could put the spectacle behind us. We'd break up again and I'd stagger back to Marie's place, and she would listen patiently, dunking her plain digestive cookie into her cup of tea, while I worried life down to a stub. Then she'd lean in and ask, "Why don't you take your hand off the bouncing ball?"

I had no idea what this bouncing ball was, or what it had to do with my life. Since I was twenty-something, I wouldn't ask. I'd go out and carpet bomb the percussionist with my love, and then I'd return from that tour of duty and have Marie put me back together again.

"You are a seeker, Deb. You are looking for something bigger in your life."

What could she see in me I didn't see in myself? I thought I was beyond repair. Even though I had read Dad's positive thinking books, taken yoga in high school, and I was in the middle of reading the Bible for a second time. I guess I was still trying to understand Christianity before I put it all away. We had never studied the Bible as Catholics. We read only the Catechism. I was forty before I learned that the first reading in the Mass was the Old Testament, and the second reading was the New Testament. Before Jesus. After Jesus. And I was going on sixty before I realized that the Torah, from the Jewish faith, was the Old Testament. But back in my twenties, I was reading the Bible and taking a lot of it literally, with a brain that was too full of chaos for it to make much sense.

"Maybe you should meditate," Marie said.

"I have a mantra already, Marie." Mom had paid big bucks for that mantra at TM. Marie told me I could use the transcendental meditation mantra if I wished, but if it didn't work, watching my breath was just fine. If I forgot to watch it, I could gently guide myself back, *back to the breath*.

"Even five minutes a day would help calm your busy mind."

Five minutes might be okay for an ordinary Buddhist, but I was an all-or-nothing Buddhist. Go big or go home. Get me to the temple of serenity and make it snappy. I began attending meditation classes at the Tibetan Buddhist Centre. Every Tuesday and Thursday, I sat for two hours.

My mind never stopped. It was like watching a catfight. The ego was peeing all over the place marking its territory. My heart raced and my body jerked around. Sighs and vocal tics broke free. Once in the middle of a sit I cried out, "Oh come on, Terry." That was the drummer's name. No one blinked. Or moved a muscle, but for me just sitting on a cushion with absolutely no movement, I broke out into a sweat. I began to think I was never meant to be a noun.

Buddhists don't pray to a deity; they believe the Buddha lives within all of us, and we all have the tools inside us to become awakened.

But when I closed my eyes, my night terrors from years ago would return. I would automatically start saying the rosary. Ten hail Mary's and then a glory be, played over and over on a loop.

Marie assured me saying the prayers of my youth were fine.

"You mean it's okay to say Hail Marys in a Tibetan Buddhist centre?"

"Just don't make your thoughts the enemy. Just watch them, then let them go."

There was a five-alarm fire inside of me. My forehead would get hot. My third eye chakra felt like it was on fire.

Stay in the moment. Come back to the breath.

By this point, I had read *Be Here Now* by Ram Dass. Or at least I had read the cover. But the title alone was a powerful concept. Up until then, I had never considered that the present day was more than something to be endured. Life felt like one long to-do list to get to the hereafter.

Occasionally, my mind would stop for a second, a minute, or maybe an hour. I would lose all sense of time. The exact feeling I had on stage. Total bliss. Pure, unfettered consciousness. I'd feel so divine after my two-hour session. I'd celebrate at the curry place below and drink some spiritual Indian wine.

As I poured my demitasse, I thought, *Indian wine is more spiritual than Baby Duck.*

Be here now.

Watch your breath.

Inhale. Drink some more.

Watch yourself date a drummer.

Watch yourself get fired from Second City.

Watch life get worse. Watch yourself get passed over by the drummer.

Breathe in. Breathe out.

Do the 20 Minute Workout *again.*

Wake up.

Join another comedy troupe.
Be funny.
Watch it all fall apart.
Again.
Again.
Again.

I'd crawl back to Marie and say, "I broke up with the drummer."

"Good for you."

"No, it's gotten so bad. Today I woke up in the Seahorse Inn with a roadie."

She'd pour me a cup of tea and say, "If you lose your way, come back, come back to the path."

TRANSCENDENTAL MAMA

The only time my mother ever looked outside her religion was the time she took transcendental meditation.

It wasn't in her nature to go far to seek. Her entire life had been lived about seven miles from where she grew up. When she got married, she and Dad moved a few miles into town and she would go out to see her parents two or three times a week. Even after that, she only lived in two other spots until she got moved into a care home. She went to the same church, the same grocery store, and she shopped at Sears until it went out of business. She was a creature of habit. For years, she smoked one cigarette a night. It was her one act of rebellion after long days of raising kids while my father worked late into the night. She did it every day until one day she woke up and said, "Well, I think that is becoming a problem." That was that.

Her youngest brother, Paul, went to India to learn meditation, and he studied with a guru who changed his name to Dustin for numerological reasons. Apparently, the name Paul was "a seven" and had created bad luck for him.

"Well, what the hell kind of name is Dustin?" my mother would ask anyone who would listen. To her, he was baptized as Paul, and he always would be Paul. Even decades later, if someone referred to him as Dustin, she and her siblings would roll their eyes.

She said the same thing when I left Napanee and changed my name from Debbie to Deborah.

"Oh, you're a big shot now."

"Mom, Deborah is just a longer version of the name you gave me."

"Okay, Debbie."

My mother discovered meditation closer to home: Belleville, half an hour from where we lived. She got the family size, signing all of us up for a TM course. I loved that we were being so avant-garde. All I remember about the training is the mantra the instructor gave me. I was to repeat it in my mind for twenty minutes twice a day, and I was never to tell anyone what it was or utter the sound in public. I'm not known for my secret keeping. When people ask me if they can tell me a secret, I say no. I cannot help it. I will blab. This is why I could never be a spy. If I were a spy, I would likely say, "Don't mention it to anyone, but I am a spy." Foreign operatives wouldn't have to waterboard me before I'd be spilling the beans. But for some reason, I kept mum on the mantra because the guru guy said it was a sacred sound, originating back to the time when sound was first created. I took the secret of the mantra very seriously, and even though I haven't practiced TM for nearly forty years, that mantra is still stuck in my head like an ear worm.

The way I remember it, the four youngest kids refused to engage in Mom's new experiment. Kevin found it ridiculous and used it as proof that Mom had lost her marbles. "What new kind of crazy is this? Replacing one form of insanity for another," he said.

The only one who seemed to go along with it was Dad, likely because Mom wouldn't feed him supper until after he'd sat for twenty minutes. He'd come home from working all day at the township, and she'd say, "Well, get to it, Jim."

"Okay, lover, whatever you say."

My dad didn't believe in TM any more than he believed in the rosary. But he did it because he loved my mother to bits and he wanted to keep the peace. He'd go into the living room and pretend he was meditating, but all he did most nights was take a nap.

I thought TM was the best thing that had ever happened to our family. It gave me hope that my mother would finally change her mind about religion, or about anything for that matter. I wasn't delusional. I didn't think she and I would ever shop at an alternative religion bookstore, but I was hoping this might mean we could have a hotdog on a Friday or stop crossing ourselves every time we drove by a Catholic church.

My optimism was short-lived because one day, she stopped TM altogether. No one knows why. Maybe she got nervous because it was too "out there." Maybe one day, she woke up and thought that the mantra was something evil, like *go eat meat on Friday*. Maybe it was her one window-shopping moment when she wanted to be a person who could meditate but just couldn't make the leap.

Kevin was the one who informed me that Mom had finally quit "this meditation horseshit." I was living in Regina at the time. According to him, one day my dad came home from work, and when he went to go to his La-Z-Boy in the living room, Mom said, "Never mind that. Let's eat." She sat down and blessed herself, and he sat too and bowed his head as she said grace. Then he made the sign of the cross and said, "Can you pass me the potatoes, lover?" and neither one of them mentioned it again.

THAT TIME I WAS
A PARTY IN A BAG

When I think about myself in my twenties, I see a shirt on a clothesline flapping in the wind. Perhaps no twenty-something has the confidence they think they have.

There were two opposite and equal winds blowing inside my psyche. One wind wanted nothing less than fame and fortune. I took classes, got headshots and auditioned for commercials, hoping the world would soon discover my blazing genius. But there was also a dark wind that tried to pull me under and drag me out to sea. I drank all night as that wind tried to keep me small and made me believe I was invisible; that all my falling downstairs and walking into walls could not be heard or seen by anyone.

Every time I succeeded, there was a part of me that would tell me I was too much, and that need to go underground has been my companion ever since. It caused me to move around so much, hide out on an island, and when Kevin was dying it almost drove me to homelessness. So many times I have come so close to toppling over the edge.

There have always been two halves of me at war with myself, and in my twenties, one part believed that if I wanted nothing, asked for nothing, and paid my dues in suffering, the gods would leave me alone and pass over my house. The other half hoped those same gods would find my hiding place and pluck me out of obscurity.

When I got fired from Second City it didn't surprise me. It felt inevitable, as if someone finally found out my secret. I was worth nothing. When they let me go, they didn't blame it on my drinking. They blamed it on the drummer. Their exact lines when they let me go were, "Why do you date musicians? You have so much potential."

Potential was what everyone told me I had in spades. *Why are you so emotional? You have so much potential. Why do you drink so much? You have so much potential. Why are you doing the exact opposite thing than what you should do? You have so much potential.*

As you start to exit your twenties, potential becomes old.

After getting the boot from Second City, I got hired by a comedy troupe that was called Acme Harpoon company. It was run by a slimeball who called me Puddin'. We did several shows every weekend out of town and I still had to pick up shifts at a bar on Queen Street West called The Epicure Cafe—or The Ep as we called it. One of the regulars, Clarke, was the artistic director of Theatre Passe Muraille. Serious theatre. While pounding back drinks one night, he mentioned a show that he thought I'd be good for. Inside every comic is a person who wants to be taken seriously—and when Clarke arbitrarily decided I would be good for the gig, I thought it was kismet. When I arrived at the theatre the next evening, I was greeted by the director, Helen, who wore a fox stole tossed over her shoulder. One of its eyes was closed as if it were winking at you.

Whenever Helen was inspired, which was often, she massaged her chest. Gave a good rub to her mournful tits, lifting them up off their resting places on her belly, as if her muse was hidden inside her D bosom. She took one look at me and pointed to the stage area in front of the room. In the centre of the area was a round object that looked like a flaccid bean bag. On the side was an unzipped opening that spanned three feet.

"Get in!" Helen ordered.

"What?"

"In the bag. You're the party, right! Climb in there and make party sounds." I must have looked stunned because she continued. "In the bag. A party, you know. Laughter? Clinking glasses? Come on! Aren't you the Second City gal? So be funny! That's why Clarke picked you."

At this point, most people would have been insulted and left, but my self-esteem was so low, I felt honoured that Clarke had thought of me for such a role. I climbed in, zipped up the flap, and lay on the floor. Inside I discovered plastic wine glasses. Party favours and blower horns were sharing the space with me. I dove into character with wild abandon and whipped up some mighty fine party rhubarb.

When I didn't think it could get much worse, I heard the door to the theatre bang open. I unzipped my pouch, peeked out, and saw a guy wearing a black boa, purple leg warmers, and Capezio dance shoes. He dropped his leather tote with a dramatic flourish and double-kissed his way around the cast.

"I am sorry, darlings, I am late! Helen. I'm Evan. Where do you want me?"

This is when Evan found out the bad news. He was commanded to the party in the bag, and like me, he and his low self-esteem climbed in.

They say there are no atheists in a foxhole, but the same could be said for two people stuck in a party bag. I was praying not to pass out, and Evan was praying in his own way too. "Jesus fucking God, the stories we will have when we go to the afterlife." Given the air quality inside the bag, the afterlife might have been closer than we thought.

For the next hour, we sat in the bag, as the cast stopped and started their lines, interrupted by Helen and her gyrations and ludicrous insight; which brought on a case of the giggles. Evan and I laughed so hard, I farted, coincidentally at the exact moment Helen and her bazookas had stopped pontificating.

Trying not to laugh or inhale, we heard the room go silent. Then footsteps. The bag was unzipped, and Helen and the fox leaned in and screamed, "Are you two going to take this seriously?"

This made everyone in the room laugh so hard that Helen dismissed us. "Come back when you can get real."

We walked over to The Ep. We needed a drink. Drinks. Plural. Always plural. We both knew we weren't going back to that show, and no one would expect us to, but in your twenties, you make a meal out of every hiccup in your life, so we spent the next two hours drinking and defending ourselves.

"I believe in my art, right? I would die for my art," Evan said.

"I've died on stage comically, but in this case I think we could have actually suffocated."

"I only took this gig because I thought I'd get exposure."

"Exposure? What exposure? Evan, we were inside a bag!" Any performer knows the only exposure you get from gigs like these is frostbite when you can't pay the rent.

A little later, Clarke came in with Helen and her entourage. We chugged a couple of boilermakers to get up our nerve to quit. When Helen went to the washroom, we sashayed over to tell Clarke we were withdrawing our names from the soirée-du-sac rôle. But before we got our resignation out, Clarke said, "Look, I was just about to come over and talk to you. Helen said she's taking the party bag in another direction."

We were being fired.

Evan and I slunk back to our table, furious. "How dare she say we were not good enough to be a party in a bag," Evan hissed. Helen returned to her table and even though she never once looked our way, we were convinced the fox was giving us the evil eye.

When we were lubricated enough, we staggered over and did a three-minute improv for her. Helen stared ahead, refusing to make eye contact. We threw our heads back and laughed uproariously. We party-bagged her. We party-bagged her hard. Evan began yelling at her, "We are being a 'party,' Helen! We have parties everywhere we go, okay?" I was so drunk I was no longer speaking English.

After Evan had finished his diatribe, I slapped the fox across its face, and Helen grabbed her moody mammaries and screeched, "You two are barbaric hacks!"

Being called a barbaric hack is probably the best insult I have ever received in my life. I still pull it out when I want to level someone else. But this second job loss had shaken my confidence. Being fired from Second City was bad enough, but being fired from the party in the bag? How much worse could this life get?

Two weeks later, as I was finishing up my shift at The Ep, Evan swished in. He had gone to the show because Clarke gave us comps for opening night, but I wasn't going to give up a shift (or my dignity), so I sent Evan to report back. He stood still in the middle of the bar and yelled across the room what I wanted to hear. "It was wretched!" Then he flitted over and whispered, "But I have bad news. The new party in the bag was hilarious! Two Ryerson students but those kids stole the show."

"Stole the show? How could two people in a party bag steal the show?"

"I don't know. But they got a standing O. To make matters worse, they used the farting bit."

"No! Don't tell me they stole my farting bit! Are you kidding me?"

"No. And it killed."

"Maybe we should have stayed and sucked it up. Maybe this was our one chance."

"I know. There are no small parts. Just small actors."

DANCING WITH A GORILLA

There's an old joke about addiction. "Addiction is like making love to a gorilla. The gorilla decides when you're done."

By the end of my twenties, I headed back to church, but this time in the basement for a program of recovery. The basements are full of repentant addicts while the pews upstairs are close to empty. I sat in a circle and said I was an alcoholic, but I didn't believe that admission at all. When I heard the words come out of my mouth, it felt like I was lying. I thought this was yet another dramatic story I'd made up to draw attention to myself.

Early sobriety is lived in dog years. One day seems like seven. A week is two months. After three weeks, I wanted a hero cookie. I devoured popsicles, ate ice chips, drank buckets of water that seemed to get sucked up in the desert that was my being.

I'd wake up optimistic, but after my first coffee, the wheels would start coming off the bus. At noon, I would walk to a church basement and share the secrets of my dark and tortured soul, and when I shared, I sounded like I was doing stand-up. Even though I thought I was bleeding out, people would tell me I was a card—a real hoot—and I had no idea why. Then some old guy would come up and say, "Keep coming back," which is code for

"You're crazy, Kimmett, so keep coming here because you'll never make it out there."

By the time I had walked to the corner, I'd fallen apart. My sanity had a very short shelf life. I was like Tarzan swinging from one group session to the next. In the middle of a circle I was safe. But ten minutes in the real world, sanity darted away again. I had chanted the rosary for years, then a TM mantra, but now it was "Keep it simple" and "One day at a time" repeatedly. The OCD was working for me.

I had no boundaries—no place where I ended and another person began. That adage "You're only as sick as your secrets" did not apply to me. I had no secrets. I would share the gory details of my drinking and debauched life with the postman. I couldn't wait to tell people I was not drinking. When a waiter asked if I wanted to order a drink: "I'll have Diet Coke because I am an alcoholic and I have a three-fold illness that is physical, spiritual and mental. I don't drink, but I tip well. Ha. Ha. Ha."

By day, I was all mouth, reciting one hilarious story after another. Then at night, I'd get into bed and replay the small infractions of my day. I would apologize to people just for existing.

Recounting the drunk nights, the raucous donnybrooks, the hitting and slapping, the police pulling the car over—the war stories—didn't fill me with any shame. They were my badges of honour. What tore me to shreds was when people who I respected saw who I was when I was drunk.

Like that time I was in a play, and after a cast party, a well-known playwright had driven me home and had to help me to the door of my apartment building because I was too drunk to walk on my own. And as he turned to leave, I grabbed him and started kissing him. "Stay the night." The men I begged to stay with me were numerous. (In early recovery, I counted them like sheep to help me sleep.) But the shame came from remembering his red fists around my hands, pulling me off him, mumbling, "You're too much, Deb."

How can I be too much and not enough in the same breath?

Like that other time, when I was at a friend's house for dinner. They had made a fabulous Greek dinner of souvlaki and rice with tzatziki and Greek wine. They were social drinkers. One drink and they felt light-headed and stopped. I had made it a practice to never drink with amateurs. But on that night, I made an exception. *Wine with dinner? Why, yes, please! How about a Bloody Caesar? Don't mind if I do.* Within two drinks, the obsession sat on my shoulder—*Why are they taking so long to pour me another?* I spoke too loudly, eager to top up their glasses.

I tried to match their rate of consumption. After dinner, my friends offered me a Grand Marnier. One small shot—measured, for God's sake—in a brandy snifter, the way civilized people do. *Christ, that glass has more room in it. Keep pouring. Don't be so cheap.* When they went to the kitchen to make coffee and plate the dessert, I went over to the bar, took the Grand Marnier bottle, and began chugging it. I had the bottle up to my lips when they re-entered the room, and my friend said, "Oh, would you like another drink?"

Without missing a beat, "Why, yes. But only if you are."

Perhaps they hadn't seen me.

At night, my thoughts tortured me. And by day, they were so loud I was sure people on the bus could hear the crazy in my head. I thought I might be too crazy to be in a recovery meeting, and now that I had finally found my people, they might kick me out.

But I need not have worried.

Do you know how crazy you'd have to be to get kicked out of a church basement filled with addicts? They aren't Mennonites. Addicts might key your car, but they would never shun you.

STUCK

The church was jammed to the rafters. Catholics and Protestants stuffed into suits they hadn't worn since the last funeral. My cousin Jay had died. He was a helluva guy sober, but when he was drinking, he turned into a scrapper. He'd take on anyone that looked at him, the bigger the better. Twenty-six years old, cute as a bug and dead by suicide: a shotgun to the head in the local TV station's parking lot.

I kept my eyes closed throughout most of the service. People likely assumed I was crying, but if you had gotten close enough, you'd have smelled moral superiority oozing out of me. I had been on the wagon for a whole ten days. Better than that, I'd lost some weight—eight-and-a-half pounds, to be exact. Mostly from bloat. I was thinner, drier and more sanctimonious.

I had gone on the wagon because I'd come-to with a man who I didn't know on top of me, hitting me. When he saw tears rolling down my face, he stopped.

"What's wrong, baby? I thought you were into this."

"What gave you that idea?"

"You told me to spank you."

That didn't sound like me at all. But I didn't remember what I had said or what his name was, or why there was an empty bag of Hostess potato chips stuck to his ass as he bent over to put on his pants. If the painting of my grandma's farm hadn't been on the wall, I wouldn't have even known I was in my apartment.

Within minutes this no-name man left, with the exit line, "You need some serious help."

Fuck you. Maybe you need serious help. You are sleeping with someone as messed up as me. Ever think of that, buddy?

I woke up more and more in strange places, asking for things I didn't want. Blackouts? No. Brownouts were more like it. One minute I was there, and then the next the floor opened and sucked me away for twelve hours. In one reality one minute, and the next minute another, with no memory of what had happened in the in-between. Time-travelling. Once I found myself barefoot in an alleyway out in the west end of the city, screaming to God, "Kill me, you mother! Put me out of my misery!"

After the spanking incident, I stopped cold turkey *again*, and now I was sitting at Jay's funeral. Maybe he hadn't meant to pull the trigger at all. Perhaps he, like me, had time-travelled through some kind of brownout and woken up in heaven, wondering what had happened.

The Catholics might not believe this, but I was convinced God sends you to heaven if you kill yourself in a blackout. The priest said, "Offer each other the sign of peace." The people shook hands and hugged and cried. The congregation knelt back down; I laid my head on the back of the high-glossed wooden pew in front of me—it smelled like Varathane. An altar boy jingled a bell, and like

Pavlov's dog, I stood up to get in line for Communion. My legs forgot that I was no longer Catholic.

As I walked past my mother—Johnny was her first cousin's boy—I kept telepathically hearing her yammer at me.

Her: *You're not supposed to go to Communion if you are not in a state of grace. You can only receive grace if you have confessed. What size is your ass? Have you lost weight?*

Me: *How do you know what I've been up to, Mom? Maybe I had already confessed in another parish, ever thought of that?*

When I got to the front, the priest pulled the Communion wafer from a golden chalice and placed the Eucharist in my hands.

"The body of Christ," he said. The statue of Jesus was hanging on the cross above the sanctuary.

I put the host in my mouth. I looked up at the stained-glass window. *Did that statue just move? Did Jesus just wince?* I tried to swallow but the wafer got stuck at the top of my mouth. *No! No. Jesus is going down, breech.*

I had been terrified of choking on Jesus from the time I received my First Communion.

When I was six years old, the old priest—the one before this one—was holding up the Communion: "The body of Christ." I was kneeling before him in my white Communion dress in white socks held up by elastics. Plaques of psoriasis covered the backs of my legs. I was up there alone because the rest of the class had made their First Communion the previous week.

On the morning of the class Communion, I had gotten so nervous that I started throwing up. I had to make my sacrament alone the following week. As my parents watched on from their pews, the priest stuck the host in my mouth—I gagged. He had cigarette fingers; I recognized the smell of Belvederes from when my grandmother tried to teach me to smoke. I gagged and choked, and people laughed.

Now, at Jay's funeral, I was standing there thinking the same thing I had thought then: *Why do I always have to make a spectacle of myself? Jesus, please don't let me choke on your body, Jesus.*

I could feel my mom's eyes on my back like she knew that the host was stuck to the roof of my mouth. *I knew you'd be back.*

Suddenly and without provocation, the wafer dislodged from the roof of my mouth and slid down my gullet like a horse that knew its way home.

THE GOD
OF YONGE
AND BLOOR

I was standing at the subway station at Yonge and Bloor, two months into sobriety, and I felt worse than I had in the first week. I don't know whether it was the oily smell of tar coming off the tracks, but suddenly I had an overwhelming urge to get plastered.

I had been doing what I was told. I called a sobriety mentor, Sue, every morning after the debacle following Jay's funeral. I had made it through the wake and funeral without temptation, but the next day, I got up and decided to drink one small bottle of wine. After that, I broke into my neighbour's apartment to steal more wine, then ended the evening by sleeping with a guy from my Grade Ten French class. A guy who was getting married the following weekend. Quite the nightcap. Despite knowing that drinking had been the root cause of that mess, I was still worried about how I was going to get through the birth of our Lord without rum.

"What am I going to do at Christmas?" I asked Sue.

"First off, it's only October."

"Well, what about Halloween? How am I going to stay sober on Halloween?"

"Isn't that a candy holiday?"

"No, that's a dress-up-as-a-horny-devil-and-get-shit-faced holiday. What if I get asked out on a dinner date?"

"You can have the man and the food, but you can't have the booze."

To be honest, I wasn't sure if I could have the man. I had never gone out on a date without alcohol.

What if, now that I was sober, I found out I don't like men? What if I was gay and didn't know it?

This was what we said back then. We had this belief that somehow you could hide your sexuality from yourself.

"Let life unfold," Sue said. "Breathe."

Breathe. Why was everyone always telling me to breathe?

"Live in the day."

Every morning I'd call her with my neurosis du jour. A part of me thought I was doing her a favour, phoning her up and entertaining her with these problems. Her responses were never what I thought they would be. She laughed when I was crying and when I made jokes, she'd say, "You sound angry."

"I'm not angry."

I hung up on her more times than I can count yet she never quit picking up the phone. Drunk, I was quite pleasant, but without alcohol, I was a ball of white rage. For years I felt I could wipe out Planet Earth with that radioactive rage.

My body ached. The connective tissue screamed out, "I'm going to die."

"No, you are not going to die," Sue stated. "You won't remember half of this stuff by the end of the month."

She was wrong about that. I wouldn't remember half of it by the end of the conversation. Sue told me I needed to be less self-centred.

"You need to think about someone other than yourself!"

I am not much, but I am all I think about. Sounds like a country song.

I started pretending to care about other people, even though I didn't. When I called, I started asking Sue how she was doing, even though I didn't give a sweet fig about how she was doing.

"How is your day going, Sue?"

"Well, I am just having a coffee, looking at the birds outside in the birdhouse."

Birds? Poor sweet Sue. Is this how small life gets? When I get old like you, will I be sitting in my housecoat drinking my coffee, watching fucking birds? What's next? Managing an ant farm?

As she burbled away, I would say "uh-huh" and "that's nice" in the appropriate places because that was what she did when I called her. I sounded like I was a kind person, but I was counting the minutes until I could go back to talking about myself.

Every moment of listening to her seemed like an hour.

She would say, "If I could give you a pill to get through this, I would, but I can't. You need to get through this by yourself."

When I became sick of her platitudes, I'd go to Marie for tea and digestive cookies.

Marie didn't understand the mechanics of addiction, but she was delighted that I had quit drinking. "See? You have finally taken your hand off the bouncing ball." A potted palm plant was beside her chair and one of its huge leaves hung in front of her like it had taken over her face.

"Can I be honest?" I said as I sipped some of her tea, "I have no idea what that means!"

She stopped and stirred her cup of Red Rose brew. "What happens when you take your hand off a bouncing ball?"

"I don't know. It stops bouncing, I guess."

"Exactly. Take your hand off the chaos, and it stops." She took a sip and looked over the edge of the china cup like she was quite pleased with her answer.

"Well, you could have told me that a few years back and saved me all this trouble."

"You didn't ask." She smiled and got up to put on the kettle for another pot. I wanted to wipe her smile to the other side of her Buddhist face but instead, I stuffed the remaining digestive cookies into my pocket.

When I boomerang back to Sue, she told me, "You need to trust in something bigger than yourself. A Higher Power."

Oh, here we go.

Oh yes, she called it a Higher Power, but I knew what she meant. She meant God.

Let's just pretend it's a Higher Power. Wink. Wink. Then some people in white robes come out from the back and ask you to go down to the river to pray.

Every time Sue talked about the Higher Power, I snapped back, "I'm not praying to any son-of-a-bitch God."

Sue said, "I didn't say you need to pray to the god you were raised with. But you need a Higher Power that works for you. It could be anything. It could be a car."

A car?

"Cars run out of gas and break down on the side of the road."

"Okay, a chair, then."

What kind of person makes God something people can sit on?

You want me to sit on God's face? Ha ha ha.

All of this seemed like an exercise in futility. Something I had to put on my to-do list.

To Do:
1. Don't drink
2. Speak up for yourself
3. Create a deity

When the desire to drink came to me on the subway platform, it was not a fluttery, romantic notion of me sitting on a patio with a glass of Chardonnay; no, I was consumed by a rabid desire for a drink. A desire so strong I was drooling, gnawing the inside of my mouth. I wanted to down a bottle of hooch so ripe you could still smell people's feet stomping the grapes. The kind of brew that people drink out of paper bags in a seedy haunt at Sherbourne and Queen. I wanted to drink in a place with blood and sawdust on the floor, where people routinely choked on their own vomit.

The train roared into the station. The subway doors opened and closed, and it took off. And there I stood, lock-kneed. Fear glued my feet to the platform.

If I move, I will drink.

It made no sense, but it was the truth. I held on to the garbage can next to me. I remembered the words from the book that the shrink in Regina had given me.

Float. Breathe. Let time pass.

I breathed. I floated above my body. I uttered a primitive plea.

"Please, God! You stupid son-of-a-bitch, you! If you don't want me to drink, you will have to help me."

That was not a prayer that Father Tom would be strumming on his guitar. "Let's all rise and sing *God You Stupid Son-of-a-Bitch, Help Me.* It's number forty-two in the new hippie songbook."

As I held on for dear life, a man worse for drink, wearing no shoes and fingerless gloves, teetered toward me, and before I could sort out what he was up to, he put his head into the bin and puked. Everywhere. Most of it missed the opening.

A bit of vomit splashed on my fingers and then the stench of him hit my nose. Bile rose up in me and for a minute I thought I might be joining him in the morning's spew.

I sprang back and wiped my hand along the tile wall. "What the hell are you doing, man?"

Un-fucking-believable.

Then this guy, my sign from God, burped again and I jumped out of the way of his second hurl. A train roared into the station, and I jumped on. Holding onto the pole for balance, I could smell his vomit on my fingers. I started giving the God that I didn't believe in a piece of my mind. *What the hell? I pray to you and what do I get? A hurling pisshead. Well, that's a little on point don-cha think? Well, thanks! Thanks for nothing.*

It reminded me of an old joke: A guy falls off a cliff, and as he goes over the edge, he reaches out for a rock and holds on for dear life. He prays, and God says, "Let go. I will catch you." And the guy says, "I can't. I will die." And God says, "No. No. Trust me. I will catch you."

After several exchanges like this, the guy lets go of the rock and falls to his death. As he lies at the bottom of the canyon, broken and bloodied, he yells up at the heavens. "What the hell? You said you'd catch me." And this booming voice from above says, "I know, but you've always pissed me off."

That's what I felt like. I thought I had ticked off God for so long that I was beyond redemption. I went home, had a shower and went to sleep. I wasn't tired, but I went to bed because I was afraid I might hurt myself.

A few hours later, I sat up in bed with a start, soaking wet, and recalled that a few years before, I had puked at the same subway station. No, it wasn't the same garbage can. It was a different gar-bage can, and unlike the urine-drenched man, I smelled like Blue Jeans cologne. I was young, cute and had all my own teeth. But I had puked in that very subway station one morning, while hung over. I had been on my way to Marie's house to carp about yet another drug-addicted man I was dating.

In that instant, I knew that I was an alcoholic. I heard a click in my head. A gun that was one moment cocked and ready to fire suddenly became an open chamber and all the bullets rolled onto the table.

At that moment, the desire to drink left me.

I was struck sober.

Thirty-seven years later, I still don't know what happened. I don't know if a guy vomiting next to me was a sign. Or what some people called a "God shot." Or perhaps I was just like every other messed-up person who was looking for a sign and finding meaning from a seemingly unrelated event. All I know is in the middle of urban decay, someone puked in front of me, and hours later I knew who I was. A woman who had to smarten up and change her ways.

It was my moment of clarity. The first moment in my life I knew I had experienced grace.

INVENTING
GOD

HAVING A
CAPPUCCINO
WITH GOD

After I got sober, improving myself was my new addiction—not as damaging as alcohol but far more expensive. My bedroom was filled with hundreds of dollars of inspirational cassette tapes and books, each one promising to answer the mysteries of life. This is why they tell addicts they shouldn't have relationships in their first year of recovery: with all those books on the bed there is no room for anything else.

When Sue said I needed a Higher Power, I was hell-bent on imagining a perfect deity into existence. Drunk, I'd stagger down alleyways, screaming into the dark and getting naked with anything that moved, but now I had high standards. I was window shopping for a God that was a perfect fit for me. What if I made the wrong choice and began praying to that childhood God again? What if I was always going to be Catholic like my mother said, or Christian? Not a normal, laid-back Christian, but that kind who, out of nowhere, drops Jesus's name into the conversation. You're out for lunch and they say something like, "By the way, I take Jesus Christ as my saviour. Pass the salt." I didn't want to be like that. But I was still thinking of God as having a face.

My friends and I had this saying for any time anything was confusing to us: "Well, that will be something to discuss when I have my cappuccino with God." I loved the idea that at the end of your life, you could have a cappuccino with God and discuss a few things. Wouldn't you have a few questions about your life? And who knows: maybe that one coffee date would lead to another.

When I was trying to find the perfect deity, I pictured him in a trendy coffee shop that offered a good cup of joe. At that time, I was still thinking that God would be male. My God would look a lot like Leonard Cohen, a dark, brooding guy who wears a suit every day of the week, even when he's riding a bicycle. Every day at the same time he'd head over to the coffee shop. Every day, he'd buy one shot of espresso, which he'd pay for in cash (who wants a deity with bad credit?), and toss it back in one swallow, followed by a Portuguese tart, which he'd eat in one bite. *Only a deity could eat just one Portuguese tart.* Everything he'd say would sound like poetry. Even household chores would sound like lyrics to a song. Like, you'd get up on Saturday morning wanting to go to the mall while Leonard would harp on about "taking Manhattan and then Berlin."

On our first coffee date, I'd lead with some small talk. You don't want to jump in and lay out your crazy, not right off the bat. Get your Higher Power to think you are charming before showing him how difficult you can be. Because, if God and I moved ahead in the relationship, the crazy would begin to surface. If I was sleeping in the same house as the creator of the universe, I'd be waking up in the middle of the night to ask him what he's thinking.

But on that first date, I'd have to start with some party prattle. Innocuous questions:

"What hairdresser came up with the mullet?"

"Where have all the fondue pots gone?"

"Who was the wiseacre who thought turmeric should be put in chocolate?"

After I pounded back a few espresso shots I'd start with the more meaningful stuff.

"Did you create us in the likeness and image of you? Or was it we who created you in the likeness and image of ourselves? Because it seems to me that we human beings have always needed to invent something outside of ourselves to blame or fear. Take aliens: A lot of humans think aliens will come and take over the world. But is this just another way to avoid dealing with the actual evil that is right in front of us? Speaking of aliens, *are* there aliens? Aren't we human beings awfully conceited to think that aliens are looking to abscond with *our* intelligence? Because you've got to admit that, as a species, we're not that bright. Are we?" Nothing. "Okay I get it, you can't say. Maybe just wink once if there are aliens and twice if there are no aliens."

Crickets. This Higher Power I created would have nothing to say to me. It would be like being on a road trip with my father. I'd take a long swig of cappuccino and babble on.

"Let's change the subject. How about evolution? I don't want to step on any toes here, but could there be a deity *and* evolution? It's been scientifically proven we evolved from monkeys, right? Right? But my question is this: At what point in the evolutionary process did monkeys become people? I know, I know. Monkeys didn't technically become people, but there must have been one defining moment where a monkey was standing there, and he noticed something different about himself. A moment where he looked down and thought, *boy, something is happening here.* He still has the prominent forehead, the shelf that sits like a ledge above his eyes—but he feels different! Maybe he was born as a monkey but is starting to identify as a human. He doesn't have the word *human* in his head because he is still preverbal, but he feels like an outsider, so what does he do? Does he go through his whole life wondering why he doesn't feel like everyone else? Or, one day, when he just can't take it anymore, maybe he straightens out his

93

legs. And he is shocked that he can do this. And he walks around, strutting his stuff. And then he quickly stops and crouches back down because he is afraid that the other monkeys will think he's better than them. Then to prove he is still just one of the guys, he eats his shit. But when he does, it makes him feel bad. And then he hears a voice in his head, not God, but a first sign of language coming in a confusing series of impulses. With a bunch of grunts and groans, he cries out, 'Please help me with this problem!'

Which would be a prayer, right? The monkey was praying. But did the monkey come up with that? Or was prayer part of humanity's evolution? Or was prayer from God or was God something we invented so we would have someone to talk to?"

Then God would put down the coffee and stare at me. The monkey theory will have piqued his interest.

I'd continue, "And what if the monkey looked over and saw a female monkey staring at him? Standing there, with her paws on her monkey hips. "Hey fool, I've been standing up for years. And by the way, here's an apple." And then I'd look at Mr. High-and-Mighty's face, and he'd be completely speechless. I might even say gobsmacked. It's as if he can't keep up with how clever I am.

Which was how most of my first dates go.

I thought I was killing it in the Higher Power department, but when I called Sue to impress her with how clever I was, she said, "Leave it to you to create a Higher Power where you do all the talking."

Frankly, I thought that was a bit cruel. The God I was inventing liked listening to what I had to say. Wasn't any communication with something a big improvement? I had thought I had to be a devout Catholic or nothing. Believe in the one true church or have no relationship to the divine at all. Sue said I was mocking the whole notion of God, but I wasn't. I was simply trying to imagine that there was a different God than the one I was raised with.

All my life, I had been looking up to a God who was in the sky, up there far away, something I was beseeching and begging, and now it was like someone had permitted me to bring him down to Earth and reimagine him as someone I could relate to.

I began to believe that God was something we imagined into existence. Wasn't it a human being (or a gaggle of human beings) who came up with the image of an old guy with a white beard sitting on a throne in the sky? The Father in the middle, the Son to the right and The Holy Spirit, left, floating around somewhere. My Leonard Cohen God was a start. A revolutionary act that showed there might be a deity that I could fabricate, who would find me and my right brain fascinating.

THE CRONES OF CASA LOMA

Ruth **called herself a witch,** but she didn't make odd potions or cast spells. There were no ferrets wrapped around her neck. She was more of a pashmina-scarf-and-elegant-linen-pants type of witch—the kind of person who summoned Lakishma, the goddess of prosperity to demand Holt Renfrew have a sale. She was a white witch. Edgar Winter type of white, from Mount Royal, Quebec—old-money white. She was what you would call otherworldly, and sometimes obtuse. If she had been on the old TV show *Bewitched*, she would have been Aunt Clara, that dotty aunt who would cast a spell and end up in the broom closet. She was a brilliant portrait painter who had three boys and was married to an ultra-conservative world banker, Michael. Ruth made the magic. And Michael made the money. "He is my patron," she said.

For years, she belonged to a group of University of Toronto Jungians. Each had gone to get a liberal arts degree and then later in life gathered again to study Carl Jung, one of the godfathers of modern psychiatry, a contemporary of Freud; he gave credibility to the subconscious longings and yearnings that come to us through images and dreams. He also believed that the collective unconscious is expressed through universal archetypes—signs, symbols, and patterns of thinking and acting that we inherit from our ancestors.

Ruth knew I was seeking something more adventurous spiritually, and one day she asked me to come to her house. "You must come and dance with the crones." I didn't know what crones were precisely, but Ruth lived near Casa Loma—a castle on a hill overlooking the city—and she was so rich she had a manse that looked down on that castle. I had only been inside once. I didn't know if I wanted to dance with crones, but I sure wanted to revisit that home that was stuffed with Victorian furniture and curios from the places Ruth had travelled.

When I arrived for the first ceremony, Ruth walked me through her living room, pointing at all the figures. "That's Oshun, the orisha (a goddess) from the Yoruba religion. She is a fertility goddess. I picked her up at a market in Nigeria. She also possesses the human qualities of jealousy and spite."

The living room walls were covered with Ruth's giant portraits: wall-sized paintings of her heroes, Jung and Freud, as well as of the writers she admired, like Virginia Woolf and the French writer Colette. Brightly painted wombs in combos that Benjamin Moore would never have paired on their colour swatches.

After preliminary hellos, the crones and I tiptoed into her bedroom, past her sleeping husband and into her art studio. She directed us to sit in a circle, and then she held a knife and walked around the outer edge of the ring and called on the four directions (north, south, east and west) to close the circle. Calling on the Earth is common practice with the mystics of Judaism and Indigenous cultures. Given the Satan-in-my-underpants experience, I was nervous about what we might conjure.

We sat cross-legged as Ruth called out the names of goddesses to guide us: Hestia, Artemis and Athena to protect us. I wasn't sure what each goddess did as I had always prayed to a male god. This was new to me. I wanted to get the credentials of those goddesses before I started summoning one of them.

Ruth told us that most people imagine God in the likeness of one or both of their parents. That would mean my male god would be a lot like my dad—hiding behind a newspaper, not listening and then mumbling smart-ass remarks that were neither helpful nor funny. The female god—a goddess—if like my mother, would make me bleach the coffee mugs and spellcheck my birthday cards.

I knew nothing of Jung's premise that we all embodied feminine and masculine energy. In simple terms, the masculine was the intellect, the decision-making aspect of us, and the feminine was emotional and intuitive. Men hunted, women gathered and balanced; to be integrated we needed to make peace with both the sacred masculine and the sacred feminine.

Ruth guided us into an active imagination exercise: "Now, breathe in and out. Picture yourself taking an elevator, down one floor, down another. Watch the elevator doors open; a beautiful scene opens for you. It could be a scene in nature, a lake, a mountain. Whatever you find beautiful." My scene was in lovely woods very similar to one I had played in as a child. "Watch yourself as you walk toward a small cottage and look in, and there you see a person or an image. It might be a family member, a helper or your wiser self."

I peered into my imaginary hut. I saw a fire almost out, barely embers. I didn't see anyone around—no wise self, milling around making soup. The lights were on, but nobody was home. "Hey there. Anybody home? Anybody?" *Perhaps my spirit guide was on a break.*

As my face was smushed up against the window, from out of nowhere, a rhino came barrelling toward me. It began stabbing me and stomping the mud while speaking in perfect English: "I'll gore holes in your intellectual arguments."

I gasped and opened my eyes. When I looked around the circle, the other crones still had their eyes closed, looking beatific. As if she could read my mind, Ruth said, "Whatever you see, it's okay. Just go with the image." I closed my eyes again, and the same place appeared, and this time I was inside the living room, bleeding. And the rhino came out of the bathroom and knelt before me. Then it reached up into the sky (there was no roof) and ripped off a piece of cloud and stuffed a bit of it into my wounds, then he handed me a piece of cloud that tasted like a marshmallow.

Ruth directed us to come back up the imaginary elevator to consciousness and land in the present moment. We were then asked to go around the circle and share. The other women had epic spirit guides. One saw a leprechaun, another a wise old woman who looked like her dead mother, and Ruth saw an angel flying away on Pegasus.

Then there was me. "I saw a rhino. It stabbed me, and when I was bleeding to death, it soothed me with marshmallow clouds."

This seemed like an epic failure, but the crones loved it. They oohed and aahed. The Pegasus lady opined, "How come you got the good spirit guide?" Was she jealous? Did she wish a rhino had appeared to her?

"The marshmallow was so unique," said another. "The rhino symbolizes that your intellect is dying, and you are moving into the subconscious."

Ruth stood and opened the circle, and then she came up to me and whispered, "Your ego is being destroyed. Good work. Let's eat."

Ruth's kitchen was filled with copper pans hanging from black iron hooks, and there were three sinks. Old cheddar, blue cheese and saltwater crackers, with this new thing Ruth called "hummus"—a dip that slowly replaced the spinach version at women's gatherings—was laid out as our post-meditation feast.

Another evening, I brought along my friend Nahanni. She was from Los Angeles, so I imagined that crones and feminine energy would be right up her alley. Up until this point, the ceremonies had only included women, but for some reason, this night, two men showed up.

One was an egghead called Clive, who had on a big black cape and a pointed hat. "I am a warlock," he said with a straight face—a warlock who was a sour puss. Earlier in the day, he had bent over and put out his back.

The other guy was younger and quite handsome and was an excommunicated Anglican priest who came dressed in full vestments and sash with a five o'clock shadow. He was a fallen minister so naturally the women allowed him to take charge of the goddess ceremony. Apparently a man who you can save *and* who needs a shave is a double win. It was evident to Nahanni and me that he was a rake, way too flirtatious for the setting, verging on cloying. But the crones fawned over him, hanging on every word he said. (Months later, he became involved with one of the crones' daughters and got her pregnant.) But in this gathering, he announced that he was called by the goddesses to do healing work on the dour warlock.

Clive was instructed to lie face down on the floor while we all placed our hands above him and chanted an ancient healing prayer.

I wasn't keen to lay hands on him and neither was Nahanni. But Ruth seemed enchanted with the prospect of curing Clive. "What if we could all focus our inner power and save you a trip to the chiropractor?" She was verging on giddy.

I placed my hands above his ear, worried that my crushing doubt (and the tight five-minute comedy set I was already creating in my head) would exacerbate his symptoms. Ruth put her hands on his back. The Anglican priest said to Nahanni, "Put your hand on his bottom."

"Say what?" she snorted.

I broke into a smile, and the Anglican priest gave me the evil eye, so I bit the inside of my mouth. Nahanni put her hand above Clive's ass. We both did everything in our power not to make eye contact because we were close to losing it. A small laugh squeaked out. It sounded like a balloon losing air. I closed my eyes, pretending I was in a trance.

After about ten minutes of this, Dour Face Clive hollered, got up, and exclaimed he was going to throw up. Ruth broke the circle. "It often gets worse before it gets better," she said. Nahanni and I went into the upper bedroom and laughed into the pillows.

Nahanni wasn't coming back. "That was some crazy-ass shit." She wasn't wrong, but I found it all quite exotic. Women gathering and performing ceremonies to call up wisdom from the Earth is not new. These rituals come from thousands of years of tradition that outdated anything the Judeo-Christian religion came up with. Many of the chants sounded very similar to the prayers we said at Mass.

Until then, I had never heard of any of them. Leonard Cohen was one thing, but entertaining the idea that there was a female goddess was something wild and unpredictable, far left of my rigid upbringing.

A few years later, Ruth moved to another beautiful home on a hill about an hour outside of Toronto. She continued to hold ceremonies every June on the summer solstice. These gatherings attracted a more grounded group of women. Women who were sophisticated and savvy: gardeners, caregivers, university profs and trailblazing feminists who had master's degrees in law and art history. A generation of witches older than me had integrated their intellectual, emotional, and artistic prowess into their daily lives. Well into their sixties, they had confidence in who they were and shared that knowledge with me. The diversity of thought gave me a different story for what an older woman could be.

We'd arrive by 10 a.m. and eat muffins and croissants; we'd listen to Ruth's history lessons on how the feminine aspect of the divine had been removed from the early church and how the deep connection to nature had been eradicated. She backed up her thesis with art pieces and historical anecdotes featuring women as central figures.

If a male Higher Power is hard to find, a goddess to worship wasn't any picnic either. I couldn't pray to Diana. I don't hunt. Demeter was a gardener and I have a brown thumb. If I was going to pray to a goddess, I wanted a goddess with a sense of humour.

Try as I might to find one, there wasn't a dearth of funny goddesses. There are endless male comedy gods: Momus, Euphrosyne and the Laughing Buddha with his big belly, to name three. But just as in real life, comedy gods outnumber comedy goddesses ten to one.

I did discover one sassy goddess called Baubo, the Greek goddess of mirth. Her goddess handle was that she was lewd and sexually liberated—apparently quite the card, who liked to crack the other goddesses up. Once she got called on to help cheer up Demeter, who was depressed after Hades took her daughter, Persephone, to the underworld. Baubo (whose symbol was a vulva on her belly) shimmied up to Demeter and flashed her vulva. Everyone found it hysterical and compelling enough that Demeter let the fruits and vegetables grow again.

Now, I'm not one to criticize a sister comic. A gal in comedy does what she has to do to get a laugh. But there was no way I was praying to a goddess like that. I was now a sober woman. Flashing my kootch at people just for a laugh was exactly what I was trying to avoid.

On those summer days, after Ruth finished her talk and the crones were done regaling me with the stories of their youth, they would pass the magic wand to me, and I would make them laugh until they cried. Then they would ask me to refill their lemonade glasses because I had legs that worked better than theirs. When night fell, I helped them carry their chairs outside to the fire where the ceremony was about to start. I was not a crone. I was only thirty-one—a mere crone-in-waiting.

This was the first time in my life I ever considered that there was a feminine side of the divine—it had simply never occurred to me. Ruth showed me how deeply the patriarchal view of God had impacted me and most women; how hard it was to feel God wholly loved you when most religions declared that you as a woman are a lesser creature with no rights. I was nearly sixty before I saw that the parts of me I had tried so hard to get rid of were not sins, but part of the human condition.

I loved the stories of those incredible women. They were a generation ahead of me, and they had fought hard to be educated, holding their own in the first wave of feminism. They owned their natural talents and they celebrated mine. Up to this point, I had thought of my humour as a weakness, a mere defence mechanism; if I were to be spiritual, I thought the goal was to eventually tame it and become "serious."

These women taught me that my sense of humour was a gift from the goddesses that could be used to heal.

PILLOW TALK

That first year of sobriety, I shopped around for a deity that worked. I read the complete works of Carl Jung and watched all the videos of Joseph Campbell. I reimagined Leonard Cohen as God, and I went back to the Buddhist temple. This time it was to the Zen Buddhist temple, not the Tibetan one. Zen Buddhism is served up plain and simple, like the first week of Weight Watchers. Melba toast and cottage cheese.

In my earlier attempts at meditating, all I could do was break out in a sweat and fidget. But then I started to get the hang of it. When I got caught up in the negative story my mind was telling me, my mind would feed me the same thoughts over and over again. But when I just noticed them and did not react to them with the familiar shock and self-hate, I got some freedom from them.

On the first day at the Zen Buddhist temple, I got there early, removed my shoes and entered the meditation hall, a cavernous open room with many pillows. It was as cold as a meat locker. Frostbite is part of the spiritual awakening.

After bowing twice, I sat down on a beautiful thick purple pillow, crossed my legs, adjusted my sit bones, shut my eyes, and started paying attention to my breath. As I inhaled and exhaled, I felt my worry drift away.

After some time—I don't know how long, it could have been five minutes or five seconds—I felt a tap on my shoulder. I looked up and saw a bald, beatific man smiling and motioning to me frantically. He put his hand in front of his mouth in horror and then shook his head at me like I was a dog who had just made a mess on the floor. *What did he want from me?* He pointed to the sensei over at the door.

The sensei is the teacher. The Big Cheese. And the Big Cheese's face was dark and brooding. He looked as if he had suddenly taken ill. The bald man pointed once again at the sensei and then at me and continued to make mouthing gestures with his hands. For some reason, and I have no idea where or why this idea came to me, I thought: *Oh, I get it. They want me to be the speaker.*

"Why would they want you to be the speaker?" asked Sue when I checked in for my daily call.

"Because I am insane. The sensei found out I was a comic and he wanted to spice things up? Anyone that has met a Zen Buddhist knows they could use a laugh."

"Oh my God, you are hilarious." Sue couldn't quit laughing.

"I know. Since I was little, I was sure my remarkable, unwavering faith would gain me recognition." *Make me humble but please take a picture of me doing it.*

When I got sober many people fed this delusion by telling me that I'd been saved for a reason. "There is a higher purpose for your life, Deb," I remember one friend saying. That was one of the reasons, in early recovery, that I was afraid to pray; I thought that as repayment for this great miracle I had experienced, I would have to stand on street corners and hand out *Watchtower* pamphlets or go to India like Mother Teresa. I even read Mother Teresa's autobiography, a book which I should mention was very badly written. *Stay in your lane, Mother.*

When that tap on the shoulder came, I was sure I was being called to greatness. My future flashed before my eyes. I imagined I would be working my way into their speaker circuit slowly, starting with a modest tour of Buddhist temples in Canada, then off to foreign lands to give witty and wise interpretations of Vipassana meditation. Sure, I'd have to learn to speak Korean, but I could grab a phrase book for twenty bucks and learn enough to get by. In the time it took for me to stand up, all these thoughts went through my head. All in a matter of thirty seconds. Sixty at the most. I straightened out my shirt, leaned in and whispered in the monk's ear. "Sure, I can speak; how long do I have?"

The man in the orange robes looked confused, and he leaned in back and whispered, "Could you please move to another cushion?"

"Pardon me?"

"You are sitting on the sensei's cushion. Could you please move?" I looked at the sensei, and I looked at the monk. Back at the sensei. They both were glowering at me.

Sue laughed so hard she could hardly breathe. Finally, she managed to croak out, "Your ego is astounding. What the hell did you do?"

"I smiled and bowed, then scanned the room for another pillow," I told her.

It seemed like every one of them was taken. All the meditators in the hall kept their eyes straight ahead. *Keep your mind on your breath. Don't let anything distract you from your practice. What practice? I don't even have a practice.* I went over and sat on a standard-issue ratty cushion on which all the regular Joes sat. The type of pillow that hurt my hips, I might add. Even though my sit bones are well padded—inherited from my mother's side of the family—sitting on these thin pieces of cotton was excruciating. Forget about kneeling and resting your whole body weight on your bent knees like some of the meditators were doing. I sat on my sit bones, legs straight out. I lowered my eyes and focused about three feet ahead of me, with my teeth chattering.

The meditators didn't give me so much as a raised eyebrow, but for the next twenty minutes, all I could do was teeter between sheer humiliation and wanting to run never to return. I remembered a joke Marie had told me: Two rabbis stand at the front of the temple. One rabbi says to the other, "I am nobody." And the other rabbi says, "No, *I* am nobody." And then the cleaner who's sweeping chimes in from the back and says, "No, *I* am really nobody." And the first rabbi turns to the second rabbi and says, "Look who thinks he's nobody."

"Honest to God, Sue, one minute I was acting like a spiritual giant and the next minute I was thinking I am a nobody."

"Well good for you. At least you didn't leave. That's a step forward."

"It was ridiculous. Everyone started singing in Korean and I mumbled along, making up words. I didn't even know what I was saying. So, I sang *sna sna sna*—you know the sounds you make when you don't know the song?"

As Sue was sniggering along with me, I became overwhelmed with emotion. There was a time in my life when I wouldn't have found this funny. I certainly wouldn't have told Sue or risked having her laugh at me, and Sue concluded the same thing at the same moment I did because she said, "There might be hope for you yet."

REPENT

The second time I saw Preacherman in front of the scone place he was reading from the Bible upside down. Preacherman was always there from 7 a.m. to 9 a.m. without fail, then he took off for breakfast and came back for another round of hollering in the late afternoon. I was half jealous that he could keep his crazy on a tight schedule like that.

I recognized the words he was spouting from the book of Leviticus. After all, I have read the Bible twice in my lifetime, once in that winter of my discontent in Regina. Leviticus was a downer. The Eeyore of the Old Testament. He claimed that God told him that two guys should not lie *with* each other. I always wondered if Leviticus had a hearing problem and maybe God had said two guys should not lie *to* each other.

Mid-sermon, a wind came up out of nowhere and Preacherman's fedora blew off and he jumped down off his soapbox to retrieve it. As he bent over, I could see a word tattooed around the back of his head. I squinted to make it out. *Repent.* What a long word to have stencilled on the back of your scalp. That was a lot of ink and hours in the chair.

As Gus and I walked away from him, I replayed the word over and over on a loop.

Repent.

Repent.

Repent.

When it was time to make amends to Kevin, I really wasn't looking forward to it. We had never gotten along, and thinking of apologizing to him made me nearly vomit. I remember he was living in Ottawa and I called him from Toronto. At that time, it was expensive to make a long-distance call. Something you put in the weekly budget.

When he picked up, I launched in without so much as a hello. I blurted out, "Sorry I hit you with a frying pan." Not when I was drunk but when I was babysitting when I was thirteen. I was always babysitting—helping out with three of the younger kids for free. Kevin was always such a pain in the ass, torturing and bullying everyone, never doing what I asked him to do. For the life of me, I couldn't make him mind me. Nobody could. I'd lost it on him. Over and over and over again. And so one night I hit him with a cast iron frying pan on his ass, over and over and over again.

"What the hell are you talking about?"

"Remember? I hit you, and then I made you a grilled cheese sandwich so you wouldn't tell Mom. And I am ... I ... er ... um ... just wanted to say I was sorry."

"Go fuck yourself." Then he hung up.

Okay then.

Making amends like this won't work. My motives were wrong. I had just wanted to get the sorries over and done with. The apology couldn't bypass the truth that I didn't like him. *Not really.* No one in our family did. And I don't know why. He had been a beautiful little boy. He had a great wit, which was celebrated when he was out in the world, but in our family, he got cast as the freak from the get-go.

Neither Mom nor Dad bonded with him the way they should have. We always thought it was because he was born into a house of sadness. Mom's best friend, Erma, had died when Mom was pregnant with Kevin, and then he was born just two months later. Before Erma died, Mom and Dad moved my sister and me in with her family and took care of her kids too. After all the work, exhaustion and pain of that experience, Kevin's birth could have been cause for celebration. Someone dies, then a baby is born. But it wasn't. Somehow, this beautiful baby became such a disappointment quickly, and he was on the receiving end of most of my mother's fury. Despite the fact he looked exactly like my Dad, tall and lanky, Dad didn't seem to take to him either. Dad would shake his head and say, *If you had any luck at all, it would be bad.*

My parents picked on him, and then we, his siblings, followed suit. If you asked him the time, he told you how to make a watch. Scientific.

One time, when we were in the car on our way somewhere, my baby brother Paul asked, "Oh Mom, how does God make a rainbow?"

And Kevin, not understanding the intention of a rhetorical question, mused, "A rainbow is a meteorological phenomenon that is caused by reflection, refraction and dispersion of light."

In a brilliant childish rebuttal, we yelled, "Shut up, you freak!"

In some families, his insights would've been valued. Maybe not by his siblings, for brothers and sisters always pick on your weaknesses, but at least by your parents. But my parents kept yelling at him, "Use your head!" But using his head was all he did. Walking around, thinking his "weird" thoughts. Always distracted.

Once, he went into the attic to put something away and fell through the ceiling. His legs were dangling in front of my mother, who at the time was sitting on her chair in the living room, reading the latest book by her favourite author, Erma Bombeck. When she recounted the story, she'd say, "I was sitting there trying to get one blessed moment of peace when this donkey (aka Kevin) fell through the ceiling. I looked up and yelled, 'Why don't you ever use your head!'" Of course, I mocked him in song. I sang him the Tony Orlando song "Knock Three Times" on the ceiling if you want me. Another time, he got asked to weed the rose garden, and he pulled out all the roses. "(I Never Promised You a) Rose Garden" followed soon after.

But the truth was he *was* smart, just not our kind of smart. Dad called him book smart. In our family, "book smart" was an insult. The Kimmetts were street smart. We bragged about how little formal education we had. We were smart in a bullshit-baffles-brains way. We didn't need facts to win an argument.

Were we mad at him because he was more intelligent than we were?

He was obtuse and did not pick up on social cues. He couldn't read the room. He told us endless stories that went on and on with nary a punchline in sight. Kevin's brain contained arcane facts about a subject you had no interest in. When he'd back you into a corner at a party, you couldn't escape. You would yawn and cough and nothing got through to him. One night, I went to my bedroom to get away from him and he followed me and sat at the end of the bed talking to me until I fell asleep.

We weren't mad at him because he was smarter than us. No, we were mad at him because the worst thing you could be in our family was boring.

That initial apology was when we were in our thirties. After that, I saw him at all the big family events, baptisms and

Christmases. My sister and I wrote a skit for his wedding. A whole *Sound of Music* reprisal. So many times, I thought I had fixed what was wrong, but no matter how many inroads we made, we always defaulted back to what we knew: indifference.

I was always giving him an internal eye roll. I thought he was beneath me, somehow. But with his brain tumour diagnosis, there was an expiry date hanging over us, so I wondered if it was too late to change anything. *What on Earth could I possibly do to fix what had been wrong for so long?*

Days after I'd seen Preacherman reading Leviticus, the word stencilled on the back of his scalp was still pulsing at me like a neon sign above a roadside strip club. *Girls. Cocktails. Repent.*

When the phone rang, I saw Kevin's number come up on the screen. I looked at the phone, debating whether to pick it up. Conversations with him were always a long-winded recounting of his life. When my kids were little, most times I let it go to voicemail. On the odd occasion when I did speak to him, I watched the clock the whole time.

Preacherman, a man in the middle of a mental-health crisis, wasn't likely an oracle sent from on high, but I picked up the phone on the fifth ring and said, "How are you doing?"

"Well, I have a brain tumour, but it's all in my head." I laughed. *Good line.* I asked him about the last surgery he'd had, and he began. "They cut an egg-sized hole out of my brain, so now I know I am about to seize because the sentences I am speaking will appear in front of me like a ticker tape on CNN. And then they started jumping into file folders. When they begin to turn to stone, I know I have to call for help. During the first surgery, they brought me up to consciousness for a minute, and I heard that the nurses couldn't find the gurneys, so I came up with an idea for them to get the gurneys back and said, 'Treat it like at No Frills and charge a quarter.'"

There were deficits after his failed third surgery—loss of balance and vision— but there was no deficit of humour. They were giving him chemo, and to counter nausea, a naturopath administered mistletoe that his wife had to inject just below his navel. When she bent down to give him the needle, Kevin would laugh and say, "Kiss me under the mistletoe." She hated that joke.

He could be truly funny, but for some reason I had to work hard to not drift off. I kept saying "oh my" and "oh dear" and "uh-huh," the way I had done with Sue, years before. But as he blathered on, I found myself wanting to move it along. Then I imagined Sue looking in on the scene with binoculars up to her face, whispering, "Act as if you are nice. Anyone can pretend they are nice for ten minutes."

The next ten mornings, I picked up the phone and practiced being a nice person. Several times through every call I'd hold out the receiver in front of my mouth and do a silent scream. *Shut the hell up!* Then I'd see Preacherman's scalp—*Repent.*

Around the eleventh morning, the first words out of Kevin's mouth were: "I am curious about you people."

"You people?"

"You alcoholics!" *Where was this going?* He better not bring up the damn frying pan again. Before I had a chance to say anything, he continued, "You fought a battle with alcoholism one day at a time and given what's going on in my noggin, I find that concept very helpful."

"You mean one day at a time?"

"Yes. Because all this medicine and all these opinions the experts are giving me, well it can take over your life. It seems like being sick is my only reality now. It's a full-time job. I have to be at the mercy of the next thing the doctors tell me to do. I don't want this thing to take over my life."

This thing was going to kill him. How could it not take over his life?

Then, like he was reading my mind, he added, "Well, this tumour is going to take over my life, but I want to live my life fully until I can't. Live one day at a time. I mean given your history I thought if anybody would understand it would be you."

I thought he was admiring my recovery and my ability to live in the day, so I took a breath and began to testify about staying in the present moment. "I believe totally in the power of staying in the day. Not just to contend with the negative things life throws your way, but the positive stuff, too. The present is where our power is. I don't do it perfectly, but I am a work in progress."

"No, no. Not just that. I mean given your history with your brain."

"What? My history with my brain? I don't understand."

"I mean after your bike accident, you were ... well, with your brain injury." He said the words *brain injury*, but what I heard him say was *brain damage*.

"I didn't have brain damage, Kevin. It was a head injury." My parents said that over and over to me. You have a head injury, not brain damage, Deb. *See, she's still normal. Look at her eating soup. She doesn't drool or anything.*

I was pacing back and forth, wearing a hole in the carpet. Gus woke up and, with one eye open, seemed to say, "Slow down, I am trying to nap here." I looked at the time on my laptop. Eight more minutes before I could stop being kind.

"Well, same diff." He sniffed.

"No! It's not ... I fell off my bike ... it was a subdural hematoma bleed." How had he come up with the idea of me having brain damage?

"Yes, but that accident changed who you were."

"No, it didn't." Of course it did. Before that, I was just a normal fretting child, and after that accident, I worried full-time. *But that is not brain damage, it was the making of a comedian.*

"I just meant ..." He began rambling on about something that I could barely hear. He had always mumbled, but now the tumour made him talk so softly I couldn't make out half of what he was saying.

"Speak up. I can't hear you." I looked over at the clock. I had only seven and a half minutes left, and I'd blown it.

"Oh sorry." He spoke into the receiver. "Can you hear me now?"

"Barely." I snapped.

"It's just that after ... You were different after that accident. You were more nervous; that's all I'm saying. I think your accident caused you to be ... funny."

"Which is how I make my money." Even though I had always earned a living as a comic, I always felt I had to justify myself to people who held a straight day job.

"It's not an insult. Yes, you could always make the dog laugh."

I looked at Gus, and he and his protruding underbite looked at me, stone faced.

"Dogs are not my target audience."

"Bonehead, you have to admit you were more nervous after. More anxious."

As he was telling me this, I began to build a case against him for things we weren't even talking about. *I might have been nervous, but you were a cheap bastard. You still have the first nickel you ever made. Remember when the boys were little, you charged them gas money to use your boat? You open your wallet and the queen squints.*

But instead, I took a breath, "How was I different?"

"You cried a lot. It took nothing to set you off."

"That's not true."

It *was* true. One wrong look at me, and I'd be screaming and bawling and accusing people of hating me. But I was fourteen at the time; didn't every teenage girl act like that?

Eighty-seven seconds before I can get off this damn phone. I don't think I am going to make it.

"I think about your accident a lot these days and I realized that nobody helped you. Nobody knew what to do. Or what to say, or how to help you. I am sorry about that."

He was sorry? I didn't think he had even noticed anything about me back then. He was a little brother, a big lump that slept in the sewing room. He had shared with the other boys until he got older, and then my Mom made a makeshift space where she hemmed our pants. Kevin was this angry, twisted, often cruel boy who growled swear words when you spoke to him and ate so much, we called him Jethro from *The Beverly Hillbillies*.

"What could *you* have done? You were a kid! You have nothing to be sorry about."

"I know. But I am sorry." I had spent years wishing someone would understand what I went through after that bike accident. How it was a seminal moment for me and contributed to my addictions. But now that he was offering me kindness, there was a part of me that didn't like that he was trying to comfort me in this way. *I was supposed to be comforting him. I was the helper; he was the helped. I didn't need to be pitied by him.*

Sue's voice came into my head: "Stop trying to control everything."

I breathed in and tried to lean in to what he was saying. He was sorry. Maybe he was making amends too. Over the next few calls, my conviction that I didn't care about him began to dissolve. Every time he spoke, my brain turned to pudding. What was happening to me? When they took the tumour from his head, did they take out the part I didn't like?

One day (and I can't tell you which), something changed. I did not roll my eyes. I was listening to him. Was it me? Or was it that he wasn't just talking *to me*? He began asking me about the things in my life. He stopped acting like everything I said was odd.

And I realized that we had wanted this to happen before now but we were stuck in that loop that siblings get stuck in. Death was unsticking us.

A new story was beginning.

I used to tell my writing students that every story begins with a *suddenly*. A person can be walking along and suddenly pirates land on the beach. You are walking along thinking you will always be alone and suddenly you fall in love. Suddenly and without warning God burps and creates a new universe. That is what happened that day. Thirty years after my failed frying pan apology, suddenly our story changed. It felt like I was finally meeting my brother for the first time.

WORRYWARTS

I am a worrywart. I used to blame it on my upbringing, but recently I reread my baby book, an album in which my parents recorded the dates of my first haircut and first fingernail clippings, and it said, "Debbie is a worried, fretful child." The entry was made when I was only nine months old. It appears I came into the world this way. As the doctor slapped me on the bum, instead of crying, I began fretting. *Oh no. Why are you spanking me? Why don't you like me? You just met me.*

By the age of ten, I had grown a wrinkled chasm in the middle of my forehead. "Perseverating" is what a shrink would later call it. "All you do is perseverate."

I had to go home and look the word up. An example of perseveration is someone who repeats things over and over in their head. *Perseverating and Prejudice?* A great title for a Jane Austen novel.

I would chew on something for hours. I didn't worry about just myself. Oh, no. I spread it around. If I liked you at all, I would worry about you, too. You wouldn't even have to ask. If you showed me the least amount of affection, I scooped up your worry and put it in my purse and went through it at night, while you slept.

It was in my DNA.

I come from a tribe of worrywarts. Irish worrywarts. Don't let that cute little Irish Spring accent fool you. The Irish are depressives. My grandparents on my mother's side had a saying: "Sing before breakfast, and you'll be crying before nightfall." This sounds a tad negative until you go to some parts of Ireland and realize that singing at any time of the day was tempting fate. My people came from southern Ireland; Catholics, from the clan of preventative worrying. We worry ahead of time so that when something bad happens, we are not surprised.

My dad was Irish as well, but his tribe was from the north. Protestants. Dad's family didn't believe in worrying. To Dad, there was no point in worrying about something because it might not happen, but Mom thought he could only be so lackadaisical because she was worrying on his behalf.

A case in point was our camping trips to Unger Island. It wasn't exactly an island because there was a causeway you could drive across to get there. Though we owned a cottage there, we never got to go in it because with six kids to feed, we always needed money, so we rented it out for extra cash.

The cottage we never got to stay in was five miles from our house. Our family was divided into two groups: The oldest three were the big kids and the youngest three were the little kids. The big kids would bike the five miles there every night in the summer. Often, my parents and the little ones didn't join us there till suppertime, so we swam for hours on our own because, apparently, kids didn't drown in the '60s.

I can only imagine what tenants who rented the cottage thought, being stuck beside a yard full of yahoos. We would put up two tents next to each other—one dining tent and one sleeping tent—fifty yards from their cottage. We had no bathroom, just an outhouse. All day long, you'd hear six kids (or more, because my aunt's brood of eight came too) swimming and screaming, "Mom, watch this! Mom, are you looking? MOM. MOMMMMMM!"

We would swim in the Bay of Quinte until our lungs were actually sore from all the diving and horseplay, then we would eat supper there, and sometimes we'd be so tired by nightfall that we couldn't make it home. Then the eight of us—six kids (three boys, three girls) and two parents—would pile into a mildewed tent with a dog or two and a ubiquitous mosquito buzzing around our heads.

One night a vicious storm came up. A frightening cacophony of thunder shook the tent.

As chain lightning zigzagged around us, we evacuated the tent and each of us climbed into one of my parents' two vehicles. Parked to the left side of the tents was my dad's van, with no seats in the back, only saws and wrenches threatening to behead us when we rode with him. On the right side of the property was my mother's station wagon with three rows of seats. We had two choices for where we could take cover. Should we run to the worrier's vehicle? Or take refuge in the car of the non-worrier? Four of the kids made it safely to Dad's van. Despite our best efforts, Kev and I got stuck in my mother's station wagon.

Dad's van wasn't boring that night; they were practically having a party, laughing and playing Crazy Eights. Every time the thunder rolled, Dad said, "That's okay. That's just God moving the piano." Meanwhile, over in the station wagon, we were doing it up Old Testament style, going around the rosary beads like race car drivers at NASCAR. Every few moments, Mom would cry out, "Jesus, Mary and Joseph!" Then she ratcheted it up a notch and began rhyming off a litany of saints: "Saint Theresa and Elizabeth!" These pleas were not reassuring at all. When she started on the Spanish and Romanian saints: " Miguel Allende and Anthim the Iberian", we knew we were totally screwed.

The next morning, the kids emerged from Dad's van and said, "Wasn't that fun?"

But Kevin and I exited our vehicle like two shell-shocked soldiers coming back from the Vietnam War.

God was never far from our lips, but He didn't offer much comfort.

When Kev and I chatted after our first call, on our journey to making peace we retold this story over and over again as evidence of how little faith my mother had. Condemning how she worshipped was our favourite pastime. If she was going to hold us to impossible standards, we'd return the favour. But after he died, I saw this story differently. The prayers by rote helped her from shattering into a million pieces.

That tumour took everything from him: his licence, his job, his autonomy and lastly, his worry. It took his worry.

Imagine having no worries. What would you do with all your spare time?

He might have been worry-free, but mine amped up. I thought about him morning, noon and night. As did my mom, who seemed to be on her knees more than she was standing. Her first-born son, who she yelled at not once but a thousand times, "What's wrong with your head?" was dying and she had to look on helplessly.

All she could do was repeat to me, "Why is God taking him? Why, when he is the only one of the bunch of you that is a practicing Catholic?" Normally I would've been offended and lit into her, but when I got the news that he was dying, that was my first thought too.

THE ANATOMY
OF GRATITUDE

For years I'd been writing out my gratitude list in my dollar-store journal every morning. No need for Moleskine because nothing precious or profound was being downloaded. It wasn't art. It was spring runoff, written fast in hen scratch. Instead of focusing on what I wanted or didn't have, I began focusing on what I did.

Focusing on what was good in my life didn't come naturally to me. In the early days of this practice, I only did the list so I could get to the complaining. *Yeah, yeah. I am grateful. Whatever. Let me tell you about my unbelievably shitty day yesterday.* There was a cynical part of me who thought being grateful was for musical-theatre types—folks who might at any moment break out in song in the middle of a wheat field. Quickly, though, I noticed that if I did this practice first thing in the morning it interrupted my tendency to go into morbid thinking.

Nutritionists say you should shop on the outer edges of the grocery store, for that is where all the healthy food is. The same rule should apply to your brain. Don't go deep into middle of your grey matter because you will bring forth philosophical ideas that sound brilliant but have no practical use at all. Ideas like: Capers and mint jelly might taste delicious yet usually go moldy in the back of the fridge.

At first, my gratitude list sported the classics: Canada, sunshine, my kids, safety. Having gotten through the night unharmed was not everyone's experience. I was grateful for Gus. His underbite and his reverse mullet. Party in the front, business in the back. I was grateful for coffee. I still am. Not that Tim Hortons dreck. I will never be *that* Canadian. And no fancy whipped mocha ice cream in a cup kind of drink. That is dessert. Dessert coffee is for mid-afternoon when you convince yourself that a frozen mochaccino isn't as bad as a dish of ice cream. In the morning I want dark roast, Italian or French blend, ground at a number four for an stovetop espresso maker. No pods. Coffee so thick one cup will get you through until lunch.

Correction: I am grateful for coffee with cream. Coffee without cream is useless to me. I know it adds extra fat, which I will have to do an extra thousand steps to walk it off, and it's worth it. I will not be made to feel guilty, especially by those people who put skim milk in their coffee. They ask you over to their house for coffee and then say, "We only have zero percent milk, is that okay?" No, it's not okay. In fact, if you had said "come over for a coffee with skim milk," I would have made other plans.

And I won't even start in on the ones who use oat milk—"Have you tried it? It's really quite good." They put oats and water in a Tetra Pak and call it milk. Milk comes from a mammary. It's not milk, it's porridge. Runny porridge you are pouring in your coffee.

The gratitude list sometimes turned into a comedic rant but it still changed my brain chemistry. It raised my serotonin levels, which changed my perception of things. On the days I missed doing it I noticed I would spiral into worry and fear with little to no provocation. I still have a healthy level of skepticism, but that practice forces my brain to think of solutions rather than problems.

What do I already do well? What do I already have? How is life working out for me?

I practiced this way for years and when it became something I did by rote I had to change it up. Therapists tell you putting pink paint on things won't suffice, so each day, after writing my gratitude letter, I began to list feelings of fear that I had brought forward into my day. Things that had stuck to me. Neuroses du jour. Every insult, every fear, real or imagined I had written on the menu. By giving gratitude and fear equal airtime, I began to notice a pattern. The things that had been on the neurosis list often got moved to the gratitude list, sometimes within days.

When I told Kev about my gratitude letters, he said: "Why not use the word *appreciation*?"

"What's the difference?"

"*Appreciation* is a softer, more beautiful word."

So, I tried switching the word to *appreciation*, and he was right, appreciation was more visceral. It came through my senses. I could smell, taste, touch and see all the good, the bad and the ugly of every day.

"Dear God, I appreciate the nurse who laughed at Kev's jokes at the cancer unit, and I love that he devoured the salmon-salad sandwich I brought him when I visited. I appreciate that my car works to go from Toronto to Ottawa, that the blueberry lavender scones are now back in stock, and that Helen, my neighbour in the next apartment, walks the halls and wears a towel on her head singing, 'Jesus loves me this I know, for the Bible tells me so.'

That yesterday, when I came out of my apartment, she stopped and touched my face, 'Look at you, Deborah. Where did all your wrinkles go? Your face looks like it has been steamed.'

That Marlene, the crack addict two doors down, who every

morning as I leave to walk Gus would be coming home, went through the same routine with me every day.

'Deb, are the men leaving you alone?'

'Marlene, at my age, they look right through me. I am fifty-nine. I am so invisible I could go back for seconds at the Costco sample table.' That Marlene cackles every time, like this is the first time she heard my joke."

I appreciated John, who runs the convenience store, who smiled at me. That when I went in for some half-and-half for my coffee, I would catch him dusting off the long-expired Apple Jacks. (Does anyone buy Apple Jacks anymore?) A few days after our initial encounter, I asked, "Hey John, are you behaving yourself?" and up popped a woman who was sitting on a plastic crate behind (and below) the counter.

She gave me a once-over and hissed, "John always behaves himself."

"Oh, you're his wife?"

"Oh, yes, I'm his wife. For forty years." I thought she was jealous, maybe claiming her territory, but when John turned away, she silently mouthed, "Too long. It's too long to be married to anyone." Every day I go to the store, Chey Yen whispers another secret to me when John's back is turned.

Appreciating what each day was bringing forth, good and bad, was hard work. But it forced me to stay present in a way I had never been before. And when the day brought so much pain I didn't think I could take it anymore, I went back into the past. To scan for those times when things had been so tough and yet they worked out in ways that I could never have imagined.

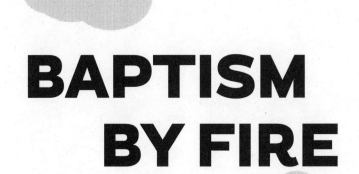

BAPTISM BY FIRE

DANNY IN THE GRAVEYARD

A **year after I got sober,** I got pregnant, had a baby and then got married. In that order.

I blamed it on Louise Hay. I bought a book she wrote called *The Law of Attraction*, which told me I had to write out what I wanted in the present tense, as if the objects of my desire had already come to me. According to the law of attraction aficionados, the future tense would keep dreams over there in the future.

I meet a man who loves me.

I meet a man in the business.

I attract a man who loves children.

Two weeks later, I met David. It started the way many long-term relationships do. He liked me and I wanted nothing to do with him. He was handsome and scrawny, and his eyes twitched because he had freebased so much coke it had screwed with his central nervous system. David was a big shot. Hyperbole was his middle name. Hollywood was his actual middle name—he changed it from Joseph to Hollywood when he left Timmins. Not only was I not interested in him, but I had vowed that I would not get involved with a man until I had had a year of sobriety. That didn't mean men weren't on my mind 24/7. I fell in love with someone new every few days. I was the one actively ignoring the guy I liked at every turn. Without alcohol, I didn't know what to do with men. I felt like a nun who had been in a convent for twenty years and was released on the dating circuit. A nun without alcohol, and with a better haircut.

When I was young, I heard my parents' generation call lemon gin the panty remover, but Diet Coke didn't have the same reputation. You never heard about people getting hopped up on aspartame and waking up beside a stranger.

The day after I celebrated one year of sobriety, David asked me to go to the premiere of a movie he had produced. This film had been made at the height of his cocaine addiction, and he had racked up a million dollars in debt. Or was it half a million? The numbers hovered above him like someone juggling plates. Now, after a little more than six months clean, he discovered he was not only "busted and disgusted," but he had made a terrible film. Like everyone in the audience, I hated the movie and wondered if I should have affirmed to attract someone who made better movies. Our first date ended back at the production house with him curled up on a couch, crying, "It's all over for me. I am doomed. I will never make it." To some women, a man lying on a couch sucking his thumb might have been a red flag. But not for me. *Let me get some of that.*

We were drawn to each other like moths to a flame. I wanted to take it slow. As we were driving home from that night, I blurted out, "I can't get involved with you. I am only a year sober."

He agreed. "Neither can I. I am only six months off coke. I am too messed up."

He drove me back to his house, and we spent our first night together.

The next morning, as I looked for my pantyhose, I reiterated, "Let's take it slow." And I never left. We were together for the next twenty years.

His self-improvement practices were more California than mine. He believed in reincarnation and past lives and aliens. I think believing in aliens is one of the requirements for people living in California. He had dropped the rosary beads of his own Catholic tradition and traded them in for crystals, which he placed on his head to open his chakras while sleeping. Now he claims he was doing it as a joke, but I will testify in court that there were flipping rocks on his head every night for the first year of our marriage. After he drifted off, I removed them for fear I'd be knocked out while I slept. He played affirmation tapes every night before we fell asleep, and despite my grumbling that I couldn't sleep with some misty tinkle guru whispering over harp music, I did wake up in a better mood.

Three months into our relationship, I became very sick. I was exhausted. Most days, I could hardly keep my head up. I was sure this was it. I was just getting my life together and now I was going to die.

Instead of going back to a doctor who would tell me nothing was wrong with me, I decided to release my energy centres by getting a Shiatsu treatment from a Japanese practitioner who was working in Toronto at a wellness centre. He was rumoured to have an exceptional talent for knowing how to read unhealthy bodies. He laid his hands on my belly and said, "Aw. Very interesting. You have a broken uterus."

I lifted my head and turned to him. "What?"

"Uterus? Is that the right word?" He pushed down on my gut like he was trying to push through to the centre of the Earth. "This is what you call uterus, right?"

"Yes. That is what I call a uterus." *I also think you may have found my TV remote.*

"Your dilemma comes from the uterus." He smiled.

If my uterus is broken, why are you smiling? I was going to die. I began to cry.

"No. No. Broken uterus. Very, very, good."

I left the appointment visibly shaken, and the next day, I went to a real doctor to get a real diagnosis. The blood tests showed the uterus wasn't broken. The uterus was pregnant.

Three months into a relationship with someone who was six months off cocaine and hundreds of thousands of dollars in debt, I was pregnant. *How did this happen? I was taking the pill.* People threw around options for me, and even though I am pro-choice, I never knew which choice I would make until I was told I was pregnant. I wanted to keep this baby. It was meant to be.

Nine months later, Brendan was born. Like all mothers in delivery, I screamed at my partner that I never wanted to do this again all the while adjusting the mirrors so I could see myself bring life into the world. David and my mother were there, and I kept looking at her for guidance. The others would encourage me and tell me to breathe, but not my mother. No, she'd nod her head and say, "I know. It's awful. It's the worst." I still love her for saying that. She had given birth to six kids and at that moment, I knew she was the only one telling me the truth.

I took one look at that wrinkled Winston Churchill face and I fell madly in love. There were those sleepless nights and trips to the doctor that all new mothers have, but to complicate matters, Brendan had club feet. One foot was going north, the other south, and each week, as he screamed while they removed the casts and adjusted his feet, I would hold his legs and kiss his sweet face.

Two months after our son was born, David and I got married in the Catholic Church. "I had no choice," I said. "David is Catholic."

People said we should have opted for City Hall. Or the United Church, but I wasn't going to be married in the United Church. They were more liberal in their ideas, but their hymns went on forever.

I pretended to be as ambivalent about the church as I was about this state called marriage. I ranted and railed that it was an outdated institution. "Women get the short end of the stick!" and "Fifty percent of all marriages fail!" were just two samples from that litany of mine. But when I looked at our marriage video, it showed a person who looked like me. A person who possessed my face and body, but she didn't look like she hated getting married. She looked like she couldn't wait to be legally wed. She didn't do that slow two-step walk up the aisle as most brides do. She hiked up there as fast as she could like she was afraid the man might escape.

As she stopped and kissed her mother on the cheek, her mother wiped away a thankful tear. Then, in a full-room voice, she made the promise to love and honour forever. She cut the word "obey" because she, after all, was a feminist. She had never obeyed anyone. She said, "I will love you forever, and I will raise the kids Catholic."

Her dad paid for the reception—a brunch at the top of the Chelsea Hotel. There were omelet stations; her mother had made the carrot cake they used for the wedding cake. While being taken out of the oven, it sank in the middle, so her mother filled the indentation with icing and stuck in one of the flowers from her bouquet. Her best friend, Deb, gave the speech, and the bride gave one of the toasts. In the video, she looked like she meant it. But if you looked closely, you'd see she had her fingers crossed for the whole thing, so if push came to shove it would all be null and void.

After so many huge changes for me in such a short amount of time, I began carrying around this terrible fear that if life got too good, God would pull the plug.

Sue would say, "Perhaps you are dying metaphorically."

What she didn't know was that on my darkest nights of addiction, I used to pray for something up in the sky to kill me. "Kill me, God. Smite me." And now that I was sober and I had a child and a husband, I was afraid he was behind on his orders and was going to finally deliver what I had pleaded for.

There was no evidence that death was on the horizon for me. Just the opposite. I returned to performing on stage for big theatres in Toronto. Second City hired me back in a different capacity. First, teaching a few times a week, and then directing and on top of that I was writing for a TV show with my writing partner, also called Deborah. I was making a new group of friends in the recovery community. I had great people around me, helping me. But there was always that free-floating anxiety that the old malevolent God I was raised on would see how well I was doing, tap his wristwatch and say, "Time's up, Deb. The party's over."

I started walking to curb my anxiety. I'd put Brendan on my back and walk for miles. I'd walk the length of three or four subway stops and we'd do errands and meet friends for a coffee. In the cold and wet weather, walking helped me let go of some of that clutter in my brain. When I walked in the winter, I used to think some of my thoughts would freeze midair, and when spring came they would melt onto other people passing by. I never walked in parks—just the streets, with the noise of Toronto traffic and a tiny companion next to me. Nature made me nervous. Even though I grew up in the country, on the outskirts of a small town on a big property surrounded by woods and a creek (or "crick" as we called it) in a time when you played outside more than you lived inside, I got jittery in wide open spaces.

We lived near Mount Pleasant Cemetery, a beautifully manicured graveyard, miles long, at St. Clair and Yonge. This vast expanse had stone benches placed along the way where people could sit and take in the sunshine. In the spring, apple blossoms filled the air, and the gardens were gorgeous. Loads of people walked, ran and biked through there, but I was afraid to enter. Ironically, not because of all the dead people, but because of the living ones. I was afraid a murderer who wanted to do me in might be lurking. The first few times I walked in there, I did a quick loop and left as quickly as I came, but within weeks, I walked farther. Soon I was able to spend a good hour in there.

Brendan slept in his pouch on my back while I explored different pockets of the graveyard that housed the graves of people from a variety of religions. Each religion respected the dead differently. The Protestants paid respect by laying flowers on top of the gravestones. It seemed the Catholics had a penchant for plastic flowers, and when I checked this observation with Aunty D she agreed. "Why would anyone buy fresh ones every week when you can get ones the rain will keep clean?" Many of the Buddhist graves had photographs of the deceased set into the headstone. On special holidays, the living would sit by the graves of their loved ones, have a picnic and offer fresh fruit, for even the dead need roughage.

One day, ambling through the graveyard, I came upon a man I knew called Danny sitting on a lawn chair next to a gravestone. I had met Danny in my first year of recovery, and he was the kind of guy who you just felt better standing next to. We'd have huge philosophical debates and I always walked away feeling like I'd been given a spiritual chiropractic adjustment. It wasn't just me he was kind to; he was one of those men who was loving toward almost everyone he met.

There was a picnic basket beside him, and he sat with his eyes closed and held a coffee cup in his hands.

"Danny, what are you doing?"

He opened his eyes and smiled. "Practicing."

I laughed nervously. "What do you mean?"

"The doctors just confirmed I have AIDS." His words hung in the air for barely a second before my mouth started moving.

"You might not die. You never know; they might find a cure."

135

But we both knew that this was a lie. It was the beginning of the AIDS epidemic, and at that time the virus was a death sentence. The cocktail was still not available. Gay men were dying in droves.

He patted the ground, and I sat down next to him and began to cry.

"I'm sorry, Danny, that you've got to go through this."

"I don't want to die either. I just know my expiry date is coming and, well, it's made me grateful."

"Really?" How could anyone be grateful for dying?

"Yes. I find gratitude is the only antidote to fear. I bring myself back to the moment and I'm grateful for everything I have at this moment."

"I can't imagine what you must be feeling. Aren't you afraid?"

"Yes, I'm afraid. I see so many people in my community furious at God. But I don't want to leave this world with my fists in the air."

"You can't blame them."

"No. Not at all. This thing is a scourge. But for me, I have two choices: I can die miserable, or I can die happy. I want to try to die as happy as possible." Then he offered me some of his sandwiches, and we sat there for a bit eating a ham sandwich in the April sun.

Again, I asked him if he was afraid of death.

He said, "Of course I am. That's why I am here." He gestured to the graveyard. "I find practicing helps me."

"Maybe I should do that. Practice dying, I mean." I felt like I was being self centred.

"No, no. Deborah, look at you! You have a beautiful baby and a brand-new husband, so you have different marching orders than me. You must practice living."

A few weeks later, Danny was admitted to the hospital at Wellesley and Sherbourne. He lay on a small cot in the ER behind a curtain at the very end of a crowded and noisy hallway. There was so much confusion about how AIDS was contracted; victims were segregated from the rest of the patients and treated like lepers, who also at one time were treated with the same cruel misunderstanding. I pulled the curtain open, and Danny lay there grey and gaunt, covered in carcinomas.

He smiled at me, grabbed my hand, and when I saw the hand almost completely black with lesions I began to cry. "Now, now, none of that," he said, pointing to the rest of his body. "This bag of bones must go eventually. Besides, this dying thing. Well, it's perfectly safe."

"What does it feel like?" I asked.

"Death? It's like a big piece of ice melting."

I hugged him. He smiled. "Aw, you are a sweetheart. Do you know how long it has been since I've been touched?" My face reddened. I didn't want a compliment for simply showing up for a human being. We held the embrace for a few moments, and he closed his eyes, and I sat with him holding his hand while he drifted in and out of sleep, then I went home and breastfed Brendan.

I grew up in a family that is schooled in the art of wakes and funerals. As a kid, my grandparents would go to every wake and funeral on our way to the beach. Grandma would say, "Wear your swimsuit under your dress because we need to drop by the funeral home and pay our respects." We'd go in, the old people would pat me on the head and tell me how I'd grown. Growing up always surprises adults. Grandma and I would kneel at the casket then she'd lift me to kiss the dead person. It didn't bother me because it was like kissing a doll. A stone doll, mind you, but paying respects like this always seemed like the right thing to do. Even if we weren't close to people, we could say sorry for their loss, bring casseroles and sit with them during those early days of grief.

As a result, when people were planning a wake, a shiva or a celebration of life, I was the one they called. I know when to speak and when to shut my trap. I know the tone you need to create in a celebration of life. It needs to be respectful, with a few appropriate laughs and a big emotional musical number. One funeral director was so impressed with me, he told me I should go into "the business." He also said that funeral directors were a laugh a minute. "If you ever came to one of our conferences, you wouldn't believe the trouble we get up to." *Stop flirting with me.*

I have performed, actually performed, at a funeral conference, and it's more about chicanery than chuckles. A lot like a car salesman conference, but instead of the latest models of cars, they are trying to upsell everything from caskets to biodegradable urns.

After Danny died, I read the work of author and guide, Stephen Levine, a man who had done extensive work with people dying of AIDS. When everyone else was running away from the pain of death, or suggesting those who were sick had somehow attracted their illness—a concept popular in the late '80s—Levine and his wife, Ondrea, showed up at hospices and sat for hours listening to people, men especially, who had been ostracized from society because of a virus. They didn't offer any answers but held space for people's pain when no one else would. The Levines' work helped me go deeper with the idea of being present and making room for the dying person to have a conversation about the death process.

I didn't know where Danny's ashes were scattered, but in the years after his death, when I was lost and afraid, I would always circle back to that tree, to reconnect to that conversation I had had with him. Touching the bark, I would feel thankful for him and all the men I had known who had died of AIDS. I would walk my infant son under the tree, eating oranges, and talk to Danny, realizing death and life were always living next door to each other.

GOD IN THE MIDDLE OF NOWHERE

When I found out I was pregnant for the second time, I was on the Pediatric wing, lying next to Brendan. He had just had surgery for his two club feet. I got up to soothe him but I got dizzy and fell. I had been anemic after his birth, so they did more blood work only to discover that my "broken uterus" was working overtime.

I was going to have two babies, a year apart.

Then more news came.

"You're a high-risk mother," said the doctor.

I took that as a compliment. *You betcha. I'm high-risk everything.* I was married to a recovering cokehead, and birth control had let me down not once but twice. What else would you call me? I was told I needed to see a specialist regularly and was ordered to "take it easy." I did precisely the opposite.

I moved to London, Ontario, to direct a Second City show. I was in my sixth month of the pregnancy when I arrived, and soon after I found a specialist there. The blood work showed that the baby was being more and more affected by my Rh-negative blood.

About six weeks into my directing job, I went into labour. I was only twenty-five weeks along. The doctors prepared for the baby's arrival; David went to the washroom and got on his knees and prayed.

I went numb. For the next few hours, faint labour pains came and went as I stared off into the distance. I was not in my body. I just thought if I pretended it wasn't happening it would stop, because a baby cannot be born nearly three months early. They knew the infant wasn't big enough to push her way down the birth canal, so they needed to do a C-section, but the hospital had run out of my kind of blood. *What kind of hospital has no blood?* They needed to add antibodies to the blood, so four hours went by before the Red Cross could deliver the correct combination. A nurse held my hand and kept telling me to take it one breath at a time.

My family began the drive to London to be with me. We didn't know if the baby would live.

When Laurel was born, she was one pound fifteen ounces. As soon as she was out of the womb, they rushed her off to the NICU: the land of transfusions and bradycardia and mini toques that had been knitted by hospital volunteers. I imagined she wouldn't live long.

How could a preemie like that live? This was 1989. I had never heard of such a thing.

But our imaginations are so limited. When I got sober, as much as I needed a Higher Power, I needed the imagination of others to see that my life could take a different turn. And now, with Laurel's birth, I needed the imagination of all the people who were helping me to see that my daughter could live.

The doctors and nurses in the NICU at St. Joseph's in London had already imagined other outcomes. Years before we arrived, scientists had imagined intricate ventilators into being and when she had multiple Bradycardias a day (when her heart stopped) nurses had perfected simple massage techniques and even tickling her feet to keep her going.

Even the pulmonary surfactants they used to elasticize Laurel's lungs had also been researched for decades. In fact, the '80s was a big time for the development of widespread use of surfactant, and though I can't recall the brand, Laurel was part of a clinical trial of a new version of the drug. We were told if she had been born in Toronto as planned, she wouldn't have been offered it.

Still I was numb and the reality of early arrival was so surreal I asked people every day to retell me the story of her birth. When I finally was able to get out of bed and maneuver my IV pole down the hall to the NICU, it had already been two days since she was born.

Knowing how terrified mothers of preemies could be, the nurses imagined ways for me to bond with her.

"Touch her."

"Tickle her feet."

"Say I love you."

I did it all by rote. I felt nothing. I tried to feel love, but nothing came.

Her head is squashed. Her eyes are taped shut.

She fit in the palm of David's hand. They cut her diapers in half. A standard-size diaper would have floated on her.

During one visit, she grabbed my finger. The nurse said, "She's a fighter." *What is the point of having a fighter if she's going to die anyway?*

They put the mothers of preemies at the end of the obstetrics hall—the area where no one congratulates you for having a new baby. There were no balloons or baby clothes. People sent Get Well Soon and Thinking of You cards. The family came with prayer books and looks of pity.

As I lay there trying to get better, my only distraction was listening to the mother on the other side of the hospital curtain turn over in bed. She had had a preemie the same night as I did. I could see her silhouette through the curtain as she stared at

141

the ceiling. We were supposed to start taking short walks down the hallway to get our bowels moving, but she refused to get out of bed—even the nurse threatening an enema didn't faze her. I admired her defiance.

One night her husband snuck in after visiting hours were over. She told him he smelled of beer, but he called her "baby" and "lover," telling her about her other kids at home. She gave him instructions on how to treat them and gave him the devil for drinking, and then they made out.

Behind that thin hospital curtain, I heard everything. I was half disgusted and at the same time I couldn't take my ears off them.

Once, on my daily stroll, I heard one of the nurses talking about my roomate at the nursing station.

"She won't touch her baby."

"Well, you know this is her second preemie. She just got the other one home after a year, and now she goes and has another."

"What's wrong with these people?"

How dare they belittle her? How dare they judge her? Don't they get it? She doesn't want to touch the baby because if she does, the baby will be real to her. If it's real, then she will have to love it and it might die and she couldn't bear to have her heart broken yet again.

After I heard them talk like that, I felt protective of her. She and I were on the same broken uterus team.

That night my roommate shuffled past me with her cigarette pack stuffed under the shoulder of her hospital gown. Instead of going to see her baby, she was going down the hall for a smoke. This was 1989, and there were still smoking rooms in hospitals. She looked at me, and I winked—the same kind of wink Grandma Brady had given me. A wink that said *we defective mothers gotta stick together.* She smiled, and a part of me wanted to hug her; the other part wanted to borrow one of her smokes.

It was then and there that I decided I would not be the object of anyone's pity. *First I was an alcoholic, then I got pregnant and then I got pregnant again.* That's what I was sure people were thinking. I wasn't going to be the loser they could look down their noses on. I was becoming a respectable person now, and I had gotten over drinking and I'd get over this. I had been through too much to let a one-pound-fifteen-ounce baby girl defeat me. I'd put on my best face and show them all how living one day at a time works. I'd rise above.

When the do-gooders came wearing their A-line skirts and their but-for-the-grace-of-God-go-I faces, I'd turn the tables around and ask them how they were doing. *This must be hard for you, being in the hospital, not knowing what to do.* I'd apologize to them for having them worry about me yet again.

When my sister came to the hospital and fainted at the sight of Laurel, I gave her my wheelchair and pushed her back to my room, an IV pole attached to my arm, saying, "That must have been difficult for you." When the Second City cast visited, making me laugh so much I winced in pain, I sent them home with my fruit basket. When David cried and put crystals on his head, I drew him to my still-swollen postnatal belly and said, "There, there honey. We need to keep it simple."

Eventually, I left the hospital, and because of my continuing poor health, I had to go back to my parents' house in Napanee. I was without my baby, five hours away from the hospital. A woman I knew in London graciously agreed to visit Laurel, and every few days, I received a handwritten note from her.

Every night, I got a call from the nurses in the NICU. In those days, the Ontario Health Insurance Plan paid for one long-distance call a day. During one of those calls, a NICU nurse innocently asked, "When are you coming down this way next? The doctor wants to speak to you." That's all that was said, nothing more. But I panicked and jumped to conclusions, thinking the doctor wanted to give me more terrible news.

I hung up and began crying. Mom told me to call back and ask them what they meant. When I did, I found that all they wanted to know was when I would be visiting next so a doctor could be on call to answer any questions. This answer should have comforted me, but it made me even more unnerved.

Every hiccup and every bump on the road threw me into a downward spiral. I was ashamed to cry in front of Mom and Dad. I'd bawled and blatted my whole life over nothing, and even though this was not nothing, I didn't want to fall apart in front of them. Plus, nothing they said comforted me. Their attempts at reassurance sounded like a reproach, like somehow I should have known better than to have a baby so close to another one. *Why do you have to do everything the hard way?* I know that neither one of them was thinking that, because they were as worried as I was, but rather than stand there with me crying and them not knowing what to do to comfort me, I asked Mom to babysit Brendan while I went for a drive.

I drove for about half an hour and wound around the back-roads up to a blink-and-you'd-miss-it village north of my parents' house. I stopped at the only store—a convenience-slash-grocery place, the last place cottagers could grab worms and beer for fishing. Maybe a Billy the singing fish plaque, before they went off the grid for the weekend. I grabbed a Diet Coke and when I came out two men were standing outside their pickup truck. I recognized one as a family friend who had been an attendant at my parents' wedding. He had gotten sober years before and had been considered one of those miracles in our family. "Oh, he was a terrible mess and then he cleaned up his life and now look at him doing normal things like a normal person." He was someone I admired from afar. His crony, a man I didn't know, was a ruddy-faced farmer who had two teeth missing, wore Wellingtons caked with manure and pants that hung so low that they showed the crack of his butt when he bent over.

They nodded and said, "How do you do?" and "How are you hanging in?"

"Good," I said.

The man I knew mumbled something like, "Well it's been a helluva time you've been having." And there was something about his country accent, and the shape of his lips, which looked like my dad's when he spoke, that stopped me in my tracks. A lump formed at the back of my throat. It was like I had gravel stuck in my windpipe and instead of a pithy reply or dropping diamonds of wisdom, I began crying, unable to offer a response.

I was out there embarrassing myself on a no-name street in the middle of nowhere.

The two men shuffled their feet and kicked at the dirt, then the one with the plumber's butt pants said maybe we should sit in his truck for a piece so I could get myself together. He opened the rusted door, which I can still hear, and got in the driver's side, and I scooched into the middle while the family friend sat in the passenger seat. There we sat in the cab of an old red pickup truck that smelled a little like a barn, staring out the window and watching no one at all go by.

All I could do was cry and ask why. "Why was I given a sick baby? I did everything right. Why did this happen?" Every time my brain tried to bring me back to order, the rest of my body protested with more wracking sobs.

For the next hour, these two unlikely companions sat there with their elbows out the window of the truck, never making eye contact, but making room for my pain. They didn't hush me or tell me to stop feeling sorry for myself. They held space. When the snot became too much, they opened the creaky glove compartment and handed me a man-size Kleenex from a dusty box that looked like it had been put in there around the mid '70s. They fed me Nanaimo bars from a Tupperware container that seemed to appear out of nowhere.

I still wonder about those Nanaimo bars. Was it just an odd coincidence that these men had Nanaimo bars in their cab, or did they always drive around with a Tupperware container full of Nanaimo bars in case a damsel in distress should drive through town?

Have I cut and pasted another Tupperware container memory into this one? I do not know. But I do know that while I sat in that truck, those two men cried too. They each had pain that usurped mine. One man had lost two full-term babies. The other had lost his son in a farm accident when the boy was about twelve. The common theme? Both told me that when tragedy hit, they had been drunk. They let their wives bury their dead and cry into their pillows while they sat in their trucks and drank themselves into oblivion.

"You are lucky, Deb. Unlike us, you get to show up for your daughter."

"But I hate it. I don't want to do this."

"Just because you are sober doesn't mean you won't be challenged by life."

I know that. *I am not naive.* But it was still shocking to me, like somehow, I didn't get that memo.

"I don't have any faith that she will live."

"Faith isn't about that. You have no control over whether she lives or dies. Faith means you get to love her for as long as she lives."

Two hours later, I climbed out of the truck, the confessional, and my head hurt—likely dehydration from all the crying. The man I didn't know handed me what was left of the Nanaimo bars and as they drove off, he yelled out the window that I could bring back the

Tupperware container when I came back to town. *When would I ever be coming back to town?*

I got back into my car and looked at myself in the rearview mirror. My face was swollen and red, and relieved. I heard myself say: "Look at you, Kimmett—you gave birth to two babies in less than nine months." *I bet that comedy goddess, Baubo, couldn't do that with her vagina.*

As I drove back to my parents, I went the long way home and cranked up the radio—only country music when you're driving the backroads. Charley Pride was singing "Kiss An Angel Good Mornin'" and the bright red sun barely peaked above the horizon— *red sky at night, sailors' delight.*

Within a few weeks of the Nanaimo bar incident, Laurel was taken off the ventilator and transferred from London to Women's College Hospital in Toronto—a few blocks from our apartment. David and I tag-teamed spending time with her and being at home with toddler Brendan. I had a Second City contract—a regular gig directing the touring company a couple of times a week. After I gave the cast notes, I'd drop by the NICU. There were fewer medical staff in there at night. I could spend time with my baby and if I had to cry, I could do it in private.

As I walked into the hospital, I passed the male sex workers who stood outside, waiting for a trick to blow so they could buy an eight ball of coke. Drug addicts sacrificing safety in a car with a stranger to earn twenty bucks. They cat-called me every night, so I began bringing them hot chocolate. Some looked like they wanted to throw it in my face. "Sweetheart look at these hips, they don't stay this way drinking that shit." Others came to expect it. "Okay, Mama, where's my chocolate?"

One night I walked into the NICU and instead of the low lights and hushed tones, the place was rocking and rolling. The night shift was having a dance party. Elvis's "Jailhouse Rock" was blasting over the speakers as a couple of nurses bopped around bathing and changing the babies while the others grooved in place as they filled out charts. One nurse was moving a child's legs and arms in time with the song as she gently washed his tiny legs. These were the healthiest of the NICU babies. For a minute I forgot where I was and I began crooning along. Suddenly I felt there was hope for these tiny angels.

Laurel was the luckiest of these, and soon she was sent home; and with every follow-up hospital visit, she hit her growth targets. Despite impossible odds, she grew into a healthy child. I could never have imagined that this would be possible. Every time she did something that a full-term child would do, I would say, "She was premature, you know?" She is in her thirties now and I am still saying, "She was a preemie, you know?"

This daughter of mine grew into a whimsical, considerate little girl who satisfied many of my requests with what would become a classic Laurel sentence: "Maybe later." Maybe later, which meant maybe never. Although often polite, she could outlast anyone in her resolve.

GODMOTHER

"A few years later, we stood next to another priest in another hospital down the street. I was telling Kevin the story of his daughter's birth. Kevin's calls now came before 7 a.m. because he was high on steroids and often sleep was elusive. Often when I was climbing out of my bed he would be climbing into his. Talking to someone when you know they are in bed at the same time as you are is an intimate act, like when you sleep in someone's bed and you can smell them on their sheets.

Before the tumour, our conversations were always a game of one-upmanship. "That's nothing; let me tell you about the time ..." Duelling storytellers. He still had stories to tell, but most days he needed me to assure him before he drifted off, so I told him stories about things I remembered about him. On this day it was about his daughter's birth.

"We stood in the NICU. The hospital lights gave our skin a yellow tinge that made us look more tired than we were. There you were, Kevin, adoring your baby who was born pink and beautiful with fat cheeks." The flushed colour was a temporary state. Before she was born, she had been diagnosed with a serious heart defect,

I can't recall the exact name—which meant that within hours of her birth, she needed to be put on a ventilator.

"She was dressed in a handmade christening gown, and she looked like a Victorian angel. The priest dipped his thumb in holy water, and he blessed this life that was so precarious." She ended up living, but at the time we didn't know if she would make it. It seemed like they had to baptize her and gave her the last rites in a one-size-fits-all ceremony.

"You were the godmother." He had picked the fallen Catholic as her godmother. "Did you lie when you said you'd raise her Catholic if I should die?"

"No, I didn't lie." When I said I'd be her godmother, I was telling the truth. I was Catholic enough, I reasoned, that if Kevin and his wife had died, in some kind of freak accident, I would have respected his wishes and raised her the way he would have wanted. Now, years later, I stood there making the same promise. "If you are worried, I will be with her and support her when you die." And I meant it.

Unlike Laurel, Kevin's daughter didn't get well quickly. Her medical challenges went on for years and she had one terrifying heart surgery after another, causing no end of grief and worry for her parents. Kevin became a good father, in fact fatherhood shaped him into someone with compassion and tenacity. He spent years of endless nights walking hospital wards, looking for signs from God like a pilgrim trudging across the prairies in the dead of winter. Yet, he showed up. "You have been a great dad."

"She came into this world as a quiet warrior, just like Laurel."

"Neither one of them suffer fools gladly." He laughed.

"Or quietly," I said.

"If they like you, they will defend you to the death. If they don't, they will hurt you!" I was glad to get him off the dark track, so I started giving my daily inspirational message.

"Don't you find these beings we give birth to, these children we call our own, had plans for us? They always tested our own limits of imagination. We blame ourselves when our kids don't do what we want them to do. We praise ourselves when they turn out all right. But it seems their lives have a trajectory entirely separate from ours."

When I finished my sermon there was a silence on the other end of the phone. He was asleep. I hung up and sat there and thought about how two sick children had given us a commonality that our other siblings didn't have. Yet until he got sick, we had never connected like this. We let our beliefs keep us separate. He believed both God and science saved our daughters. I believed that neither one would be worth much without imagination.

"But your kids are baptized?" Kevin asked. The conversations that week centred on my spiritual history.

"Brendan had been baptized right after he was born because that was during one of my I-might-still-be-Catholic moments. But when Laurel came along, we didn't get around to it for six years."

"I see; but didn't they go to a Catholic school?"

"Well, that wasn't my idea. David said he wanted the kids to go to the Catholic school and I agreed." I justified it to myself by saying the separate school had better parking than the public school.

When it came to rules, the Catholic school system was not a take-what-you-like deal. Laurel had to be baptized. When we went for the spiritual instructions for her baptism, the priest came out at 9 a.m. on a Saturday reeking of booze. In a slurred voice, he ran down the questions he would be asking us on the day of the ceremony.

The first and, I felt, the most ludicrous question coming from a drunk priest was, "Do you reject Satan?"

To which I said, "No."

"What? You *don't* reject Satan?" I think I shocked him into sobriety.

"I'm not answering that question."

"Deb, come on," said David, his eyes beginning to twitch.

"You come on, David. It's a dumb question. Who does he think we are? Satan worshippers trying to slip in here and make live sacrifices?"

David turned away from the priest and talked out of the side of his mouth like somehow that would prevent the priest from hearing us. "Just say you reject Satan."

"I don't believe in Satan. It's all superstitious bull ..."

"Keep your voice down. We're in a church."

"I can't be a hypocrite."

"Sure, you can. It's one of your best qualities."

"That priest is three sheets to the wind; maybe I should ask him if *he* rejects Satan." I turned back to the priest and gave him a talking-to. In my head. *Look, if you had asked me if I respected Jesus, and thought of him as a wise man. I would have said yes. Or, if you had asked me if I will raise my daughter to love and respect herself and others, I would have said yes ... but this Satan question is ridiculous.*

What was even more ridiculous was that I was at this church in the first place. What was I even doing here? Hadn't I said I was no longer Catholic?

Being a devil's advocate comes with a price. I wasn't allowed to participate in the ceremony—or to stand next to my kid. The priest had me stand in the outer circle of the altar just to make his point. The lapsed Catholics on David's side of the family—the ones who hadn't darkened a church's door in decades—got to stand in the inner circle. They came with gifts and rosary beads, apparently very happy to announce publicly that they denounced Satan. They stood up there and promised that if David or his devil-worshipping wife died, they would gladly take over the care of Laurel's mortal soul. I should've told them I'd see them all in hell, but that would have just solidified the drunk priest's argument.

When the ritual was over, I was in tears. *What was I trying to prove?* As I stood on the steps outside the church, I handed Laurel a large bouquet. Daisies, sunflowers and baby's breath to match her personality. She was delighted.

"Oh, Mommy, I thought only big people got flowers," she gushed.

"No, honey, in some Indigenous cultures in South America, people give children flowers to welcome them into the world." That was a total lie. A complete fabrication. On the steps of the church no less. I had no idea if Indigenous cultures in South America or anywhere else gave flowers to six-year-olds, but it seemed like a good idea that they might want to try.

After Laurel was baptized, I broke up with the church again. David and I had a sort of joint custody of the children, spiritually speaking. He took the kids to Mass one week, and I took them to the Zen temple the next. One Sunday, they recited the rosary and learned about mortal and venial sins. Next, they learned breathing and mantras. They gave their first confession at Our Lady of Perpetual Help and then did the children's guided meditations in the basement at the Zen temple at Vaughan and Bathurst. I called them spiritually bilingual, but really, I think they delighted in pitting their parents against each other.

They only liked the Buddhist temple because the service was shorter and they got to have cookies and green tea in tiny teacups. At church, the Mass was long and tedious, but afterward, David took them swimming and for French fries at Fran's.

When I tried to explain my faith journey, it sounded to Kevin like I was describing one of those murder charts, where all the witnesses are tracked on a bulletin board with thought bubbles, arrows and string.

"I've got to go to hit the hay," Kevin said. I could tell he was already there, fading quicking into slumberland because his voice was so low, I could hardly hear him, "Think up another story for tomorrow, but no sad ones, okay?"

"Okay. I will tell you some good ones."

WHAT KIND OF GOD KILLS AN INNOCENT HAMSTER?

Both David and I were raised Catholic. David had a father who drank, wreaking holy terror on them during the week, and then, on Sundays, putting them in their Sunday best and parading them out to church. I was pushing up against a Catholic mother who criticized me morning, noon and night, and had us drop to our knees to give her ten Hail Marys when we stepped out of line.

In our rebellious days, David and I had tried to escape all that insanity by dulling ourselves with alcohol, drugs and danger. In sobriety, we used that same chaotic energy to propel ourselves forward. We were determined not to go backward to our addicted ways no matter what, and that drive motivated us to explore different philosophies and modalities that would make us better than the way we were raised.

But on the negative side, that drive was a fire that threatened to consume us. The philosopher Nietzsche wrote: "He who fights with monsters might take care lest he thereby become a monster." More to the point: Don't become the thing you hate. If you don't watch yourself, you will replace your childhood dogma with another dogma just as demanding. We may have broken free of Catholicism but we spent thousands of dollars on fixing ourselves.

155

There was always one more book to read or one more food group we needed to eliminate or one more platitude to digest before we could stop and rest in our own company.

The incessant self-improvement was exhausting, and with all that deconstructing of language, our explanations for everything were never simple. Take our explanation of the afterlife, for instance. After David's mother died, I was tucking the kids in when Brendan wanted to know where Grandma had gone. The kids always got philosophical about ten minutes before bedtime. After a lengthy disclaimer on how I didn't believe in reincarnation and that heaven wasn't a real place but a state of mind, I wanted to paint a healthier alternative and blurted out, "She has gone back to nature."

"What's nature?" asked four-year-old Laurel.

"It's the land, the water, the air and the trees. She is part of the landscape."

The next night when we were eating dinner, the wind was howling hard and it was snowing, and Brendan began to cry, "Grandma must be scared out there tonight."

"Why?"

"Being part of the landscape, living in the trees, she must get cold."

"She isn't living in the trees. She's part of the trees," I said as David began his nightly tuck-in ritual. Every night, he folded in the sheets and made the kids into burrito babies.

"How could Grandma be part of a tree?" Brendan asked as David tucked in the sheets. "Is she now made of bark? Is she a leaf?"

"My mother is not a leaf, for God's sake." David turned to me. "What are you teaching them, Deb?"

I shot Brendan a dirty look. The kid always sold me out. "Don't be so literal, son. I didn't mean she's an actual leaf. I was meaning she's a seed in the karmic dance of life."

The kids didn't understand metaphors any better than most people do. "Our grandma is out there dancing?" Brendan sat up; David had wrapped his arms so tightly in the sheets he could get no traction.

"No, her spirit is dancing," I explained.

"No, Deb," David said. "My mother isn't somewhere dancing the hokey-pokey." He turned to the children. "Listen, kids, my mother was a wonderful, religious woman. She is in heaven." He dimmed the light and the celestial sky of star appliques danced on their ceiling.

"Well, you don't know that, David. Even the Catholic Church now says heaven is more of a concept than a geographical location," I said.

"No. It's not. It's a place. And if anyone is going to that place, it's my mother. She was a saint! She is not some seed out there being twisted around by the wind." Then he turned to Brendan. "Grandma is in heaven. She is sitting at the right hand of God; I can tell you that!"

"I think I am going to need an extra snack," Brendan said, then he threw himself off his bed and rolled across the floor trying to unravel himself.

"Me too," Laurel piped up. She undid the sheets, climbed out of bed and unwrapped her brother, and the two of them began padding toward the kitchen. Laurel whispered to Brendan, "If Grandma's in Heaven, I wonder if she can see me when I pee."

David hit the roof. "Grandma doesn't watch people pee. Honest to God, Deb, what have you put into these kids' heads?" Then he walked off to the bathroom to take a leak while I gave them extra cookies and started the bedtime process over again.

The next existential dilemma came when our dog killed the hamster. The hamster's cage got left open by a kid named Cody, and Shorty, our terrier, tore the hamster to bits in front of my kids and their friends. What followed was a cacophony of kids crying. Then David came to the rescue and tried to give it CPR. Not mouth to mouth. He wasn't that crazy. He just did light compressions with pinky fingers on the hamster's chest for far too long until I started chirping, "Good Lord, stop it. The thing is dead."

"Everything is not like *Lord of the Flies*, Deb. I will not give up hope." Then he grabbed his crystal, and he and the dead hamster took an expensive trip to the vet. While he was fleeced for a few hundred bucks, I was back at home throwing sugar at the problem. The kids were too distraught to eat the cookies, but I managed to consume about two dozen.

Things had almost calmed down when David came back with the hamster in a Chinese food takeout container. "Well, kids, I have some bad news for you. Fluffy has gone bye-bye."

Again they all began howling, as if this was some surprise plot twist.

That night, Brendan got in the tub and cried so loud that at one point he put a plastic bucket on his head to muffle the sound.

I had told him to do this when he swore. He used to say "shit" a lot, and I told him he could only swear in private. In response, he began putting a bucket on his head while he was in the tub and saying "shit fuck damn" repeatedly.

As he sat in the tub with the bucket on his head, crying, I was scanning my brain for the right things to say, and in a fit of desperation, I resorted to the old-school God.

"God wanted Fluffy back with him in heaven."

Brendan took the bucket off his head and wiped the tears from his eyes and got out of the tub. There wasn't even a hiccupping sob as he padded off in his Homer Simpson slippers. I thought I had finally got it right. The heaven concept was comforting to him.

I didn't believe in that destination, but for him, it was concrete proof that Grandma and Fluffy existed in a place with a postal code. And don't we all need specific answers in the middle of our grieving? But the next night, he got in the bath, put the bucket on his head, and began wailing.

When I drew back the shower curtain, there he sat with the sand pail off his head, shaking his fists at the heavens. "What kind of God kills an innocent hamster?" This is a question that many great philosophers have wrestled with since time immemorial.

Laurel took everything in and stewed about it. People called her an old soul. But my son, Brendan, was a new soul, fresh off the presses.

"Mom," he would ask, "tell me honestly. Do you think *Ninja Turtles* was a better TV show than *Power Rangers*?"

"I don't know. They were both better than that flipping *Little Mermaid* we watched a million times. Where was that girl's mother? I'll tell you where: Dead."

"Mom, if you were forced to sleep with Sailor Moon or Pink Power Ranger, who would you pick?"

"Pink Power Ranger. Sailor Moon is underage."

"Do you think Polly Pocket or My Little Pony was the worst toy ever?"

"Pogs were the worst toy ever, with Crazy Bones coming in a close second."

"Mom, I need to know if you would survive a zombie attack. Would you shoot them with a gun, or stab them with a knife?"

"I don't believe in zombies, son."

Zombies are right up there with aliens as far as I am concerned. I don't think you should give aliens or ghosts or zombies any sort of encouragement. I am sure once you start believing in them, they start believing in you, and before you know it, you're in the psych ward because every time you see a meat thermometer it reminds you of the probe they shoved in you.

But, to preserve the family's peace, I always played along with the zombie thing.

"I'd kill the zombie with a knife because I don't believe in guns."

"That wouldn't work, Mom. Zombies have incredible lower arm strength and would take the knife out of your hand, and you'd be dead."

"Then why did you give me the knife option?"

"I was testing you because I need to assess your chance of survival."

See, this is the thing about my son—he likes to have a plan. He used to get up and demand to know the day's schedule. He always wanted rules, which I wasn't great at providing. One day, after I had been out for the night, the Canadian Armed Forces called my house. The woman from the recruiting office asked for him.

"Is Master Brendan there?"

"No. He's at school."

"Well, he called last night about joining the army."

"He can't join the army, he's in Grade Six."

When I asked him why he wanted to enlist, he said he needed discipline, and my methods and his father's were too willy-nilly for his development.

I knew if we were going to get any rest, we needed to get the zombie plan in place.

"All right, then. I'd splash them with water, like the Wicked Witch of the West." My answer just made him hostile.

"If you're not going to be serious about this, we're not going to play."

"Play? Is this supposed to be fun?"

"I mean it, Mom. Smarten up or I'm not even going to talk to you."

"Really? You promise?"

I excused myself and put myself to bed before I did any serious damage.

His concerns were for naught as no zombies showed up unannounced. In the end, both kids refused to attend temple or church. Neither of them was drawn to organized religion. Yes, they were impacted by the short stint at Catholic school, but let's face it, they weren't carrying the same viral load as David and me.

Maybe they didn't need to pursue these spiritual practices with the same vigour because they were starting life from a different point than us. They have issues. Absolutely. Issues like anxiety for the world. But their questions don't seem to involve asking whether there is a God or not. When they stub their toes on life, they don't cry out for Jesus or Buddha to help them; instead, they go to their devices and yell, "Hey, Siri!"

A GROWN-UP TIME OUT

Most days, there is little holy to be found in mothering. I used to say I didn't know I was in a bad mood before I had kids. When I lived alone, if I woke up crabby, I could just take it out on myself. If I went out in that state of mind, I could be kind to friends and colleagues because, after a few hours, I went back to my own house alone. But having a family is different than even having a roommate—they never move out. The lot I was living with wanted honesty and kindness from me every single minute of every single day. I was always failing them. I don't know if I minded falling short of my ideals as much as I hated all those witnesses.

Stephen Levine, whose work with the dying had inspired me, was also a Buddhist teacher who said: "There is no one practicing meditation harder than a mother!" A truer sentence was never spoken. When you have a family, you are consistently withdrawing from the emotional bank account, and it doesn't take much to go into overdraft. After a few nights with no sleep or a bout of the flu, my relationship with my inner wisdom went out the window.

Plus, children are mean. No one warns you about this when you take them home. They just hand them to you at the hospital with no warning that they will hit, bite, walk and pee all over you while you're sleeping. If they did, there would be hundreds of children left in the hospital nurseries. They pick at you all day like birds. They back you into corners while trying to get their boots on, kicking and hollering hateful things at you. Letting them into your bed at night to sleep with you requires a bicycle helmet. I ended up in the hospital twice from my daughter hitting me in the eye with her bottle. She was nine months old and had the swing of a prizefighter. It's hard to buoy yourself up with positive self-talk when you're wearing an eye patch.

I tried to keep up with my daily practices. At night, I lay in bed and tried to meditate, but I'd doze off before the second exhale. In the middle of the night, I was the worst. Sometime around three in the morning, they'd wake up and want to play or just have a chat. I'd go off my head, spitting and spewing venom in some narcoleptic-induced blackout. "Get to bed before I crucify you." Yes, I was channeling my mom.

In the morning, I'd feel so guilty, and I'd promise myself that if they woke me up again, I wouldn't be *The Exorcist* mother, but of course I was. I never had a moment to connect back to myself. If I woke up at 7 a.m., my son would wake up too, demanding cereal. I tried to get up at 6 a.m., to get ahead of him, but he turned back his internal clock too. The only semblance of peace I got was the five minutes in the shower, somewhere between shampoo and conditioner.

I prayed on the go. Get a takeout coffee and say the Serenity Prayer on the fly. I did positive affirmations next to a very noisy dryer, and, in a desperate act for any agency over my own life, I joined the VIP section of the Y, which was double the price of the regular membership, because they had muffins and a nap room. I loved that nap room. I'd put my workout clothes on, head to the gym, get a muffin the size of my head and have a good power nap. It was the only time in my life I can say I loved going to the gym.

My head couldn't keep up with all the changes that had happened to me. In less than two years, I'd gone from being a party girl to being a super mom.

Up to this point, I had been doing everything wrong, and now I was trying to get it all right. People called me a perfectionist. *Yeah? Well for a perfectionist I am not very good at it.*

House cleaning was the thing that would do me in. The people I lived with, or "those filthy pigs" as I liked to call them, never picked up a thing, and I could hear Mom's voice in my head every time a dust bunny rolled by me. "Why is this place such a pigsty?"

I learned how to clean from my mother. If she had bowed down to one of Ruth's goddesses, it would have been Hestia, queen of the hearth, the deity in charge of dust bunnies—a relentless goddess who is only happy when you are pushing an Electrolux up a set of stairs.

When I was a kid, I hated my mom's crazy rules about housework. She had this notion that it took twenty minutes to vacuum the basement. Did she get this time from some mothers' handbook? I found it a ridiculous amount of time, so I'd vacuum for five minutes, leave the vacuum running, and spend the rest of the time hosing my body parts. I'd make vacuum hose hickeys all over my body then come up panting like I was worn out from working. She'd come over and sniff me.

"I hope you weren't down there vacuuming your body parts again?"

"No.

"Look, you better not be lying to me or you're going to hell."

"Fine." Then I'd march back down to the basement and pretend to vacuum again.

I had promised myself I would do it differently with my kids, but the same goddess ruled me. Saturday morning was the day she demanded worship. During the week, I was a mom who didn't mind a mess. I loved the art on the table and making crafts and the kids pulling the pillows off the couch to make it a pirate ship.

But on Saturday morning, there was a hostile takeover. Hestia would descend upon me with her Herculean colour-coded to-do lists. Around 7:30 in the morning, I'd enter the living room, the vacuum cord wound around my neck, looking like the head of Medusa. The kids would be splayed across the couch like their spines had been removed. David would be watching cartoons, laughing and eating Frosted Flakes dripping in milk like some man-baby. I'd start screaming. Is there anything more infuriating than seeing your family enjoying themselves when you are trying to clean around them?

"Today is the day we are going to get this under control. We are going to take the bull by the horns."

Do you know what happens when you take the bull by the horns? The bull wins.

The floor was covered in puzzle pieces and tiny furniture from Polly Pocket sets so small that when stepped on, they would make a kidney stone feel like a picnic. I began to vacuum around them and sigh (oh, the sighing!). By 8 a.m., I'd be making threats: "I am going to leave you and get my own place—a place where people like you aren't allowed to traipse dirt all over the floors—a place where I don't have to always be the bad guy."

"*Why am I always the bad guy?*" yelled every mother since the beginning of time. Every Saturday morning, I affirmed that I would be patient, but within thirty minutes of opening the bottle of Mr. Clean, I'd be screaming at them. "Just forget it! Take them to a movie!"

They'd all look at me like, "Is this a trick?"

"No, it's not a trick." If I could get rid of them, maybe I could work in peace. "And get them some popcorn," I'd yell as I watched them leave the house to go see a movie that I'd wanted to take them to, and I was left alone to scrub and bleach things, full of tears and self-pity. I didn't even care about cleaning that much. Most days, they'd be barely out of the driveway and I'd be back in bed asleep from exhaustion.

I had to get myself under control, because I was slapping and yelling at them the same way I was raised.

Sometimes I could short-circuit by giving myself a grown-up time out. I stood in the closet. A lot of friends were coming out of the closet, but I was going into it.

I found the bedroom closet the most calming. It reminded me of Temple Grandin's squeeze machine. Temple is an animal rights activist with autism who invented a machine that would contain her energy when the world felt like too much. A machine she continued to modify through her life, it was the hug Temple couldn't let herself receive. My closet was the hug I couldn't ask for. What did I do in there? Did I think of anything profound? Negative. I stared at clothes on hangers and wondered why I had ten white shirts.

Standing with my back against the wall, I'd hear the children going through the house yelling for me—"Mom! Mommy! Where are you?"—while I held my breath and prayed they wouldn't find me. The dog, Shorty, would sniff me out first and would whine while pawing at the glass. Soon the kids would join him outside, whispering about my mental state. Yes, they always knew I was standing in there. But we all pretended it was a surprise.

This was especially embarrassing when they had friends over. Especially Cody. All kids have a friend like Cody—a kid whose mother hung on every word he said like he was a Messiah. He was so pampered we were convinced he'd turn out to be a criminal. Which he almost did, as he ended up being a Senator. An Ottawa Senator for the NHL. One of the goons who took the good players out.

"Why is your mommy in the closet?" asked Cody, the future third-round draft pick, one day.

"I don't know," Laurel shrugged in her wise old woman way. "It makes her feel better."

"When will she come out?"

"Maybe later." *Smart kid.*

But Cody wouldn't leave it alone. He put his jam hands on the mirrored closet door. "That's weird. That's just weird."

So you want to talk weird, Cody? You go insane if your peas touch your fish sticks.

Motherhood is, at best, a brutal game. But it's like improvisation. If you are trying to be perfect, it's futile. I had gone from being one of the most responsible kids you could meet—a kid who wanted to get it perfect—to the most irresponsible teenager who didn't care about my safety or anyone else's, to a perfectionist mother who was driven by some internal exactitude. I wanted to make up for what I considered an emotional lack in my upbringing by making sure my kids never lacked anything. I wanted to be exactly the opposite of my mom. It was as if I'd written a script in my mind of what a perfect family was supposed to say and do, and the only problem was nobody knew their lines.

Birthday parties were over-the-top, loot bag-induced madness. Sometimes there were fishponds, and David hid behind the couch and pretended to be a shark. I'd give him notes on his performance. "You can't say 'glug, glug, glug.' What shark says 'glug, glug, glug'?"

No store-bought cake for my kids, just homemade. I wasn't bad as a baker, but decorating was not my strong suit, as my birthday Barbie cake attested. The recipe: Take a Barbie doll and place her in the middle of an angel food cake. Ice the cake with pink frosting and place sparkly silver things around the circle of the cake. The result was that Barbie would look like she was wearing a pink ball gown. But my husband bought a skinny angel food cake—half the calories and half the size of a normal one—which meant her cake dress only went up to her knees. (*If Barbie even had knees.*)

In a fit of spectacular fury, I sent my husband back to the store to get another skinny angel food cake. I'd save the day if I put the two cakes on top of each other. But the two thin cakes were still not tall enough because when I stuck Barbie in the middle, she fell over.

"Maybe you could just rip off her legs," David said.

"What is wrong with you, David? She isn't a Landmine Victim Barbie." The kids were arriving any minute, so I took his suggestion, ripped the limbs off the doll, iced her boobs, and set the cake in the middle of the table.

After a scary scavenger hunt, where we misplaced two children in a ravine for a harrowing seven minutes (one child, now thirty, says she still gets triggered when she smells moss), we got to the cake portion of the proceedings. Laurel was born in July, so her birthday always seemed to fall on the hottest day of the year, when it was about 80 degrees in the shade. The kids were drenched in sweat, smelling like the inside of a hockey dressing room, and with no air conditioning, Barbie had begun to tilt to the side. The icing was dripping off her boobs. It looked like she and Midge had been out on a three-day bender. The boys began laughing at Barbie's "boobies."

David came to the rescue. "Hey kids, would you like to see the movie that destroyed my career? I lost over a half million on that one."

In unison, they all yelled, "No. Not again!"

David pretended to cry.

"Let's watch *The Simpsons*," Brendan said.

"You're not allowed to watch *The Simpsons*," I yelled.

Brendan swung around at me and slapped his head with a "D'oh!" in classic Homer Simpson form. Then Cody shook his head. "He watches *The Simpsons* all the time, Deb. Why do you think he hits his head all the time?"

"For fuck's sake, Cody," Brendan yelled.

I didn't know he watched *The Simpsons*. I thought he was being funny when he did all his Homer quotes.

"You're not allowed to swear," Cody said to Brendan.

Well, Cody, you're not allowed to put your jam hands on my bedroom closet mirror or kill our hamster.

Then Brendan belted Cody across the head for yelling at me. I knew I should tell Brendan to stop hitting the kid, but I had had just about enough of Cody and his bad attitude. David pulled the kids off each other and, as he paraded them all up the stairs, I heard him say, "Let's watch my movie. The first hour isn't great, but five minutes in the middle aren't half bad."

I had started the day off chanting and affirming that the party would be a success, and now I was ending it standing in a closet with one fork and two skinny cakes.

Barbie and I needed some alone time together.

COMMENTS FROM THE PEANUT GALLERY

"Your stories never lose any flavour** in the retelling, do they?" Kevin had asked for funny stories and now he was dissing them. "You got one crazy-ass brain."

"We are not bringing up my brain again, are we?"

"I'm just saying your brain zigs and zags. No wonder Mother didn't know what to do with you, freak." *Didn't you get the memo? You were the freak, not me.*

"Kevin, she didn't know what to do with your brain either."

He paused. "Can I tell you something? You look just like her."

Low blow. I knew I looked like her. Some days I'd look in the mirror and see my mother staring back at me and I'd think, *How did you get in there?* But is there anyone in the world that wants to be told they look like the person they've had the most trouble with in the world? "Well, as long as I don't act like her then that's all I care about."

"Deb, you have to find forgiveness for her, you know." First, he says I look like her and now he has the nerve to tell me to forgive her.

"All I have done for the past twenty years is try and forgive her."

"Have you tried therapy?"

Therapy? Of course! Yes! Listen to my psycho babble–laced conversation. Wasn't it obvious that I had been paying people to listen to me for decades?

I was always going to one expert or another. I'd had a couple of drive-by therapists since the first guy in Regina. I'd go to one or two sessions and I pour out my guts, then race off in another direction. All the while never telling them I was a comic. If you told a therapist you were a comic, they started telling you jokes or saying you used humour as a defence mechanism. To which I always replied, "Well you use pretending to care as one." One woman thought I was a singer in another life, hence my penchant for dating musicians. I paid yet another guy fifty bucks to hypnotize me so I'd eat only twelve hundred calories a day. I binged on Scotch mints before I got to the street.

Then there was the forensic psychiatrist who David and I went to for marriage counselling. He had worked on many high-profile murder cases in Canada, so naturally we thought he'd be good for us. David stopped going after the first session because the man wanted to see me alone. If you want to know the state of our relationship, David and I stood outside his office, arguing.

"He likes you better," David said.

"No, he doesn't. He thinks I am a psychopath."

I continued marriage counselling alone. Week after week I went in and finally got the courage to tell him that I had spanked my kids. He turned to me and said, "If you hit your kids, I am obliged to call child welfare services," so after that we didn't talk about me or my problems. We turned out attention to his high-profile cases. One visit he showed me turn a picture he took with Vinny the Mauler right before after they sentenced him. "It's not the best picture. Vinny looks good but I look a little bloated, don't you think?" Vinny had murdered thirteen people but he was "not criminally insane. Of course what he did was nuts but to get off on a criminally insane defence you need to not know what you are doing. Vinny plotted and planned these murders." Then he paused and looked at me like he was looking down the barrel of a gun. "Don't kill your family, Deborah, because I can tell you right now, you'd never get off on a criminal insanity plea."

I was insulted by this.

You just met me. You don't know how nuts I can get if I put my mind to it.

The doctor and I got along just fine if we discussed his career, but it all went to hell the day I asked him, "What kind of therapy is this? Is it Jungian, or more the Adler approach? What are we doing?"

He stiffened and said, "That is none of your business."

Why isn't it "any of my business?" I have a right to ask about my own care. But of course, I said nothing. I couldn't confront this guy or anyone at that time. I could never say what I needed to say. I smiled and said he was right, and then we made another appointment and I never went back. I didn't quit. I didn't call and cancel the appointment. I even paid the missed appointment fee. *I'll show him.*

"Kevin, I've had years of therapy!" *Decades.*

"Yes, but did it help?"

THE
GOLDMAN
SESSIONS

SESSION #1

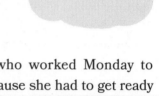

Goldman was a petite woman who worked Monday to Thursday and took Fridays off because she had to get ready for Shabbat. At our first appointment, she sat down and adjusted herself in her chair. "Would you like to sit or lie down?" She pointed at the couch.

"Lie down?" If I laid down I might never have gotten up. "I'd prefer to sit," I said.

"Tell me, what brings you in today?"

"Well, nature abhors a vacuum, and so do I."

No response. Nothing. She looked at me like I was speaking another language.

"I mean I hate cleaning."

"Oh, I see. You're coming to therapy to stop vacuuming?"

"No. I want to stop yelling and going crazy when no one cleans up the way I want them to."

"It can't just be about the cleaning."

"It is about cleaning. It's about fairness. Nobody does any housework but me. I have tried to accept that. Suck it up. I have prayed and turned it over."

"Turned it over?" Goldman looked confused.

"You know, turned it over, like ... gave it to God. Let it go. Let it be. I have been sober for several years now, and ..."

"Sober? You quit drinking?"

"Yes, I'm an alcoholic."

"When did you *start* drinking?"

"At sixteen. Look, I've already dealt with that part of my life and ..."

"Sixteen? That is so young. Why did you start drinking so young? What happened to you?"

"Nothing. I'm from Napanee. Everybody drinks there. Listen, the reason I'm here today is I want to be nicer. I can be nice for about twelve hours a day, then I lose it."

"Twelve hours a day? That's pretty good," she said. "What does 'losing it' look like?" She continued, making air quotes.

"It includes screaming, yelling, cleaning, changing the rules, and ..."

And it includes spanking my kids.

I didn't tell her that. There was no way I was going to tell her that. Especially not on my first visit. If I'd learned anything from the forensic psychiatrist, it was to keep my mouth shut about the thing I most needed help with.

I stared at her and said nothing.

Goldman smiled at me, and she too said nothing. Then she waited until the discomfort was so bad I was forced to say something. *I hate silence.*

"I know what you're thinking. You think this has to do with my childhood."

Therapists love going back into your childhood so they can figure out all the reasons for your pain. I figured I'd help us both by speeding up this process.

"Look, I had a good childhood. My dad worked three jobs to make ends meet. He is a kind man and has had a lot of big ideas in his life. He worked with his hands, but he's a great thinker. He's ill right now."

"What's wrong with him?"

"Heart issues. And he had surgery a few months back, and, well, he's not back to normal."

"This must be hard on top of everything else."

Of course it was hard. The good die young, but the miserable last forever.

Right on cue she asked, "Is your mother alive?"

"Oh, she's alive, all right."

"Healthy?"

"As a horse. Nothing will take her out. If there was a nuclear holocaust and the whole world was reduced to ash, she'd be the only one to survive." Five minutes in and I had already started on her. I didn't want this session to go south like the one with Father Tom, who wound up forcing me to stick up for her, so I threw in a few positives. "She's strong. She started as a school teacher, but she stopped teaching when she had kids. Then she opened a paint and wallpaper store selling Benjamin Moore paint in our basement."

"So she was a business woman?"

"Well yes. Maybe. I am not sure if she liked it or not. But her contribution was called pin money." Pin money. A British term that came into vogue in the 1970s when it was still being used to reassure people that a wife wasn't overtaking her husband's earnings, but rather that any cash she might earn was unnecessary and frivolous.

"Dad even named it Kimmett's Kolour Korner with 3 K's."

"Three K's? As in KKK?"

"No, look, Dad wasn't like that. He is a great guy, but when he got his bright ideas, he never factored in nicknames. Later in life, he owned a burger joint called Big Jim's. People shortened it to BJ's."

"What does that mean?"

"Never mind. Look, he is a good guy. He is my everything."
Even though I was not lying on the couch, salty tears flowed into
my ears. "No, no. I had a good childhood. We were outdoors playing all the time, building forts, playing in the crick."

"Crick?"

Damn, my hillbilly roots. That Eastern Ontario accent was
trespassing onto city land.

"Creek. We ran up and down the *creek* and played so hard and
built forts, and it was a good childhood."

"Yes, you have said that." She smiled some more. I looked out
the window again.

I turned to her. "Can I ask you a question? When I was nine
months old, I developed psoriasis. What was that about, eh? Eh?
What do you think that means? Do you think I was picking up
stress from the anger in my mom?"

"Maybe you were allergic to cow's milk."

"I'm not allergic to cow's milk! Or gluten, or nightshade vegetables, and I don't have psoriasis because I am nervous."

"*Are* you nervous?" She asked.

I chanted. My bedroom was full of self-help books and there
was hardly room in the bed with my husband's crystals. *Of course
I was nervous.*

"It has covered 89 percent of my body since I was an infant. All
I am saying is I didn't make myself get psoriasis."

"Of course not. Psoriasis is an autoimmune disorder."

I continued, "But because I had psoriasis, I was dragged to
shrines where they prayed for me. I was treated with tar baths
and sunlamps. I was hospitalized twice for thirty days in Kingston.
Once when I was five and once when I was seventeen."

"At the age of five, your parents left you in a hospital for a month?"

"They didn't *leave* me. It wasn't abandonment. We lived in
Napanee, and the hospital was in Kingston, thirty miles away, and
they only had one car."

"But I'm sure as a little girl, you missed them. You were only five. It's okay to have missed them," Goldman suggested. "And you said there was another time you were hospitalized?"

"Yes, when I was seventeen. I spent another month in the hospital. Psoriasis again. But I went home on weekends. Today, it would have been handled as an outpatient case, but I was admitted back then. I loved being in the hospital because after I did my UV lights and tar treatments and oatmeal baths, I got to leave and walk around the park, which was right next to the psych hospital. In the afternoon, I'd walk around the park and pretend I was mentally ill."

"You were pretending to be mentally ill?"

"I sat in the sun and did my homework, and if someone came near me, I talked to myself. Is it weird that I'd rather be in a hospital than at home?"

She was writing furiously. "Can I go back for a minute? You were taken to shrines for this? I'm sorry. What are shrines supposed to do exactly?"

"They are a place where you pray for miracles."

"Miracles?" She gave me the same piteous look the Regina shrink had when I'd said despair was a sin. "And given tar baths and taken to shrines ...?"

"Then I was in the hospital again when I fell off my bike and got a head injury..."

"Uh-huh ... and then you began drinking?"

"OK, well, I don't know. Look, those two things aren't connected. It is not like that."

"What's it like then?"

"Maybe I was just born a freak. Or I brought all this neurosis in from another life? Do you think this freakishness came with me from another life?"

"I don't believe in reincarnation," she said. "I find this life hard enough to deal with without worrying about past lives I can't remember living."

That was something we could agree on.

Goldman stopped writing and gently put her hands to her lips and said, "All right. Our time is up. I'd like to see you two or three times." Then she stopped.

"Two or three sessions? And then I will be okay?"

"No, no, no. I want to see you two or three times a week." She paused as she pulled out her calendar. "What days will work for you?"

"I can't come three times a week." *Who am I, Woody Allen?*

"Okay, we will do it twice a week to start."

"To start? How long do you think this is going to take?"

"Let's just see, okay?" She stared at me again. "Before you leave, is there anything more I need to know about you?"

"Yes, I'm funny."

"Really?"

"Yes. I'm freaking hilarious. You must not fall for that, okay?"

"OK. Noted." She jotted a couple of sentences in her book then looked up over her glasses. "I will see you Thursday."

For the next two years, I went to see her twice a week, and all I did was talk about my mother and my childhood. And Goldman only laughed once.

SESSION #12

"**I**n Grade Six,** I began keeping track of Mom's moods. She found my notes in the back of my notebook. I made charts of her bad and good moods. I thought Wednesdays were her good days, but then she'd surprise me and be mad on a Thursday."

"You were looking for a pattern?"

"Yes, but I couldn't find one. On Wednesday, she was happy, and then the next Wednesday—well, everything would go off the rails. I constantly wrote about her. Her moods. I wrote plays and skits; she knew my pen was dangerous. Mightier than the sword. She found that writing and started after me with a fly swatter."

"Did your mom hit you?"

"Yes. Sometimes. It didn't bother me. I mean, I didn't like it, but everybody got hit in my day. Spanked."

"I didn't."

"Really?" It never occurred to me that not everyone had spanked their kids. "Was that because you were ... Jewish?"

"No."

"The hitting didn't bother me much because it was over and done within a few minutes, but the constant criticism is what destroyed me. It never ceased. You could never figure out when it was going to come at you. "One day you'd get complimented, the next insulted for the very same action. Most of all, I was always criticized for my imagination." A girl with an unfettered imagination is always too much for a mother who got taught early in life to expect nothing but hard, cold reality.

"When she wanted to hit me, I just ran away from her. I was taller and faster. But the roiling anger. Christmas and special occasions were the worst. She'd start with the cupboards and the cleaning closets ..."

Aha! This is where the closet obsession began. I am making real progress in diagnosing myself.

"We'd scrub and bleach and declutter and bake, and all the while we had her raging at us. It wouldn't be Christmas if she wasn't crying and going to her room."

Goldman was mystified. "Is cleaning the closets a Christian tradition?"

I laughed. "Um ... yes. We clean to prepare for the baby Jesus."

"It sounds like she put a lot of pressure on herself."

"She tried so hard to get it right, to give us the 'perfect' Christmas. The Christmas she never had. And now, I'm just as bad. I am ruining my kids' lives too. Maybe ruining holidays is part of the job description of being a mother."

Goldman again smiled. "Or perhaps mothers can't win for losing."

SESSION #28

"Dad died last week."** I flopped down on the couch and lay down because I was too exhausted to sit up.

"Oh. I thought he was getting better."

"Yes, no, it turned out that on top of the heart stuff he had lung cancer." His illness had been long and drawn out, and his death was not unexpected, yet I was gutted, especially when Mom started giving away all his belongings. "My mother is already cleaning out his stuff. She even got rid of all his clothing."

"Perhaps having his stuff around is far too painful for her."

Still, the man she loved for forty-eight years was barely cold in his grave when she divided up his things between us—the six kids. One of my brothers got his leather jacket, which had "Goodyear" on it because Dad had been instrumental in bringing that company to our hometown. Kev got his ski sweater.

"My inheritance was three pens with no ink and a beer-bottle opener."

Goldman looked confused. "What? But you don't drink!"

"Exactly. Three inkless pens to a writer. Wouldn't Freud have a field day with that one?"

"Freud was an idiot," Goldman blurted out. "He hated women."

185

"Oh, Dr. Goldman, don't you think that was a passive-aggressive move? Giving me, the writer, three inkless pens! Come on. That can't be a coincidence."

"Maybe they were cheap pens."

"Of course they were cheap pens. Dad never bought anything that was good quality."

SESSION #56

The Spanish have a saying: when a child is born, they show up with a loaf of bread under their arms. I think my daughter, Laurel, brought me a pen and a notepad. About a year after she came home from the hospital, I began writing about her extraordinary entrance into the world. I had written every day for years, but up to this point, I had only written sketches and comedic turns for TV, but not a full-length play. I'd been an improvisational actress and writer at The Second City, and then in a comedy troupe with my best friend, Deborah Jarvis. We called ourselves *The Two Debs*. The two of us travelled the country doing sketches, and we did some writing for TV. But these were short pieces that hadn't lasted more than a few minutes.

I began to write a fictional play about my real premature daughter called *Miracle Mother*.

At the time, our apartment had no space for a desk let alone a room of one's own, so many evenings after the kids went to sleep, I went to my mother-in-law's house to work in her basement. The ceiling was so low I hit my head on the way up and down the stairs.

My brother-in-law lived down there in what became known as "the bunker." He had temporarily separated from his wife because of one of his drinking episodes. He was sober, but he was operating on rage and adrenaline. He got up at 3 a.m., so he went to bed by 7 p.m.

He would keep the bedroom door open and lie on the bed, and I could see him in his boxer shorts swearing at the TV. "Fucking CNN." Then he'd malign the book he was reading. "Fucking *Handmaid's Tale*." All he did was swear. And occasionally come out to go to the loo, and as he did, he'd snort, "I hope you're not as boring as that fucking Margaret Atwood." *Who wouldn't kill to be as boring as fucking Margaret Atwood?*

I laid the track for the first draft, and Tarragon Theatre in Toronto commissioned my piece. They also assigned director Annie Kidder, who helped decipher my notes and started helping me shape my ramblings into a workable stage piece. Her instructions were to be brave enough to tell the story as it was. Besides delaying punch lines in this more extended form, I had to learn to trust my truth, but I was dogged by doubt. The poet Rainer Maria Rilke, said, the voice of doubt never hollers, it only whispers, and mine sounded like a fly buzzing around my ear in the early morning. *My story was not dramatic enough. My baby had gotten well, and many babies as premature as Laurel stayed sick! Don't I need something more intense? Sadder? More dramatic? Someone less me!*

There was a great divide between improvisation and the "regular theatre," and now that "regular theatre" had accepted me, I was sure I needed more significant plot points, grander imagery, and where was my symbolism? Annie convinced me that the story (and the symbolism and imagery) would emerge organically.

What emerged was not a medical story, but a story of a woman named Kathleen window shopping for faith; a woman torn between her family's traditional religion and her husband's new age philosophies. Kathleen, who was very closely based on me, sat on the fence spiritually, not knowing what she believed. I eventually became comfortable with what I had written. Even my brother-in-law in the basement liked the first draft.

But when I saw the rehearsal, I freaked out. Watching actors perform my life, I felt violated. *Who permitted them to steal my story?*

I had gone into a room, fumbled around in the dark and created something. Now that light was shining on it, I saw how truthful the beast called fiction is. My brain became a snowstorm of anxiety. I wanted to take my emotional ball of wax and go home. After each run-through, I would take Annie aside and tell her the actors needed to speak up.

"Tell them to move faster. It's like they are talking in slow motion."

She reassured me they were nearly yelling, and that they'd look like the Road Runner if they moved any faster.

I don't have a poker face. I have a *why the hell would you do that* face. The actors avoided making eye contact with me at all costs because if they happened to look in my direction I would be frowning or mouthing the words as they spoke, or making faces as they said their lines. Finally, it was "strongly suggested" that I take a break from coming to rehearsal.

"Your job is done now, Deb," said Annie. "Why not let us surprise you on opening night?"

The mother of a one-pound, fifteen-ounce baby needs no more surprises.

On opening night, Urjo Kareda and I listened to the show on the monitor in his office. In the second drawer of his desk, chocolate, booze and smokes were what he referred to as the Urjo Kareda Opening Night Emergency Kit. I lit up a cigarette, and Urjo turned up the monitor.

"Why are they mumbling?" Urjo wondered.

"You can't hear them either? I knew it. I knew it," I replied.

Despite my inability to hear the words, there was laughter. In the wrong places, I might add. I had cried writing the piece, so it was horrifying to hear that I had somehow made my tragedy a regular riot.

The newspaper gave the play good reviews, but it was as if the critics spoke softly in a small font. Urjo took me out for lunch at a fancy-pants restaurant, telling me, in short, that I was the next big thing. Theatres in Canada and the States wanted to produce the play. This was it. I was going to be a rich and famous playwright. A wealthy playwright is an oxymoron, but I was riding high on hope.

I heard through the family grapevine that my mother had come to see the play. She and my dad had driven from Napanee to Toronto to see it without telling me. I called to ask what they thought of the piece, and my dad, who had answered, said, "I'll let you speak to your mother." This was the same trick he pulled when they found out I was pregnant with Brendan.

As he passed the receiver (and the buck), my mother informed me she was very disappointed in me and my play. "You could have written something that would have made the whole experience of Laurel's birth the miracle it was. You should have written something nice."

Likely Van Gogh's mother did the same thing. "Vincent, for God's sake, leave your ears alone for a minute and paint some nice sunflowers."

Mom didn't see my work as art. "There is no truth in that piece."

"I took artistic liberty. I never said it was a documentary."

The play was a fictional version of the truth, about how a premature birth kicks off a debate that rocks a family's faith. (As does a premature death from a brain tumour.) As the main character, Kathleen, searches for her version of spirituality, she challenges her mother's rigid religion. After the two duke it out, they both understand each other a little bit more.

It was what I called the best-case scenario.

Mom said, "You have made a spectacle of me and everything I believe in." I flashed back to my first psychiatric test in Regina, and that question: "Does your family find you strange?" It should have also asked: "Do they find you offensive?"

I justified all the choices I made. "Mom, I wrote the best version of things. I wrote it as a template for what our relationship could be."

It didn't comfort her. I don't know why she came to see the play—she is a private woman. She hates anyone knowing about "her business." When we were kids, she bought a new couch, and when the Sears truck pulled into the driveway, she quickly shepherded all six kids into the house so we wouldn't go outside and blab to the neighbours about our big purchase. "You don't need to be broadcasting that we are getting furniture." It was a couch, for heaven's sake. We weren't in the witness protection program. And by the way, our neighbours might not have been that bright, but I think the Sears truck in the driveway and the delivery men carrying a couch wrapped in plastic would most likely have tipped them off. Since purchasing a sofa was top secret, I knew telling the story of a family overcoming addiction and wrestling with faith would be too much for her.

Even though I took liberties, it wasn't a lie as she said. Quite the opposite. It contained far too much truth. We didn't speak for what seemed like ages. *Was it a month? Six?* I fired my mother. Or she fired me; I am not sure. And as was so typical of our family, neither one of us informed the other of their termination.

We weren't speaking, but she had set up camp in my head, yammering at me every waking minute. Every morning, I woke up, and we'd start in on each other in my imagination.

"I get to write about what I want. This play was about me trying to understand my own trauma."

"You don't get to write at my expense."

This is how all wars start. Two people shadow boxing with each other, thinking their ideas are better than the other's.

SESSION #64

"**N**ot all the pens you buy work," Goldman noted. Yes, I was still going on about the damn pens. My therapy was covered by our provincial health care system and hours and hours of taxpayer money was spent talking about three pens.

"Of course, but maybe one pen would have no ink. Two? Okay, maybe! But three pens with no ink? What are the odds of that? She did this on purpose."

"Maybe your Dad was the one that wanted you to have them."

"I doubt that while Dad was dying, he looked at the pens with the words Richmond Township on the side and said: 'When I die, make sure to give those pens to Deb.' No, if he wanted to bestow pens to me, he would have given me his stripper pens." My father had a collection of ballpoint pens with pretty girls on the side. When you turned them upside down, their shirts came off. I could see my dad wanting me to have those. He would have said to my mother, "Give those girly pens to Deb. That will make her laugh." But during the last few weeks of his life, he wasn't thinking about what my inheritance would be, was he? No. He was too busy gasping for air.

Before he was taken to the hospital, I spent the night watching him struggle to live. Mom was worn out and had gone to bed.

"I need my sleep, or I will go crazy." She took out her hearing aid so she wouldn't be disturbed. I can still see him sitting in the chair in the kitchen with his red long johns on and his barrel chest. He leaned so far forward that he looked like he might topple over. The next morning, the oxygen people brought in so many tanks, it seemed we were going scuba diving.

He said, "When they bring the oxygen, the game is over."

I said, "I know people who've lived for years with oxygen tanks."

I looked at Goldman. "Why did I say that?" She said nothing but lifted her butt cheek. "I didn't know anyone who even used oxygen tanks. I lied because I thought it might help him have hope. As two insomniacs, we spent that last night together—both of us pacing. He went up and down the hall, with me picking up his oxygen tank cord so he wouldn't trip and hurt himself. At one point, I told him he needed to rest. When he was settled under the covers, in his bed, I played him a guided meditation by the metaphysical teacher Louise Hay, who said, 'I am a good person. I am enough. I have enough. I do enough.'"

Goldman lifted her other butt cheek. *What was she doing? Farting?*

"Well, your heart was in the right place," she said, lowering her bottom back on the chair.

"How can you say that? The man's lungs were filling up with fluids, and I was doing affirmations. I still see my haunted father's face, gasping for air. How could he believe he was a good person when breath was beyond his reach? 'Deb, I have to keep moving.' That's what he said. He paced the rest of the night. I don't think my father had ever walked that far in his life. He was the kind of man who would take the van to get to the end of the driveway to get the mail, so by the morning when the ambulance arrived to take him to the hospital, he was done. I still see him sitting on the gurney, spindly twig legs hanging down; the paramedic came and helped lower his head on the pillow." I fiddled with my fingers. "She hated my first play. Did I tell you that?"

"Yes, you mentioned that several times ..."

"Hated that I was creative." I sounded like I was a trial lawyer trying to convict her. "I wrote a murder story when I was fourteen and when I read it to her, she shook her head and said, 'That didn't happen.' Of course, it didn't happen. It's a murder story. If it had happened, she wouldn't be sitting there reading it because the mother in the story was based on her, and that mother was dead."

Your honour, she criticized me as a child. She came to my play and didn't like it and now she was giving me pens that didn't work and a beer-bottle opener. I paused and looked out the window.

"I know why she gave me that beer-bottle opener—because she wanted me to drink and become drunk and then not have enough ink to write about her anymore."

Goldman lifted her butt cheek again and then took in a deep breath, "Grief is a prickly companion. It will twist minor infractions into full-blown legal cases against those you claim to love," said Goldman.

"I know what you're going to say: She is my perfect teacher. That I 'attracted' this kind of mother." I don't know why I was even saying this. I no longer believed in this kind of nonsense. But I thought she might, so I began spitting out the jargon as a preemptive strike. "I find it hard to believe that I was some soul in outer space window shopping for a bad mother. Don't tell me I wanted a bargain-basement mother to help me transcend, okay? I can't handle that, okay?"

Dr. Goldman handed me a tissue. "I would never tell you such a thing. She hurt you. But she is hurt too. I want you to grieve all that she couldn't give you. Only then will you truly be able to let it go."

I lay on the couch and blew thirty-two years of childhood into my Kleenex.

SESSION #83

66 ❚ have something to tell you. It's not pretty." Given the stuff I confessed to her, I don't know why I thought this story was the big reveal. "When I get overwhelmed, I stand in the bedroom closet and hide from my children. They walk around the house looking for me and I just stand in there." I told her the entire story. How I hated my kids, how I hated fucking Cody. How I couldn't stand hamsters in my house, the whole enchilada.

Without even looking up, she asked, "How long has this been going on?"

"Ever since I brought my kids home from the hospital." *Be serious, Deb.* I looked at her and said, "I stood in there because I wanted to spank them. I mean ... er, I did spank them. I spanked them on the ass. Once. Twice. I slapped them in the car. I try to ... well more than that, I threatened my kids. I am so scared that I am going to ... hurt them, that sometimes I'd just get so mad and scream, so I stand in there until I can get myself ... under control."

"That was a wise move to calm yourself down."

"I look like a fool."

"Well, it's better than hurting them. Do you still spank them? I mean now?" Goldman stared directly at me, and I shook my head.

195

No, I didn't. It was true. I had wanted to, but my temper had been diminishing by coming to her twice a week. I had stopped a lot of my yelling, too. After a second, she leaned in and said, "I used to stand by the dryer in the basement. Sometimes I stood there for a half hour as my children went through the house looking for me."

"Really? You did?"

She nodded and looked at her watch. "Time's up. That will have to wait for another day."

SESSION #112

The rage left with a whimper, not a bang. On that last day of therapy, Goldman sat on a different chair opposite me and told me what I meant to her. She told me that she celebrated the growth in me and recited what she believed I had learned. I reciprocated by telling her how much she had contributed to my life.

Marie, my acting coach, had taught me that I was a spiritual being on a path despite my screw-ups. Ruth, the rich witch friend, had taught me that creativity lived within me and that my intuition wasn't something to be scoffed at. Goldman undid a whole lot of conditioning I had been raised with.

In two years, I learned that a lot of pain had been created when I was a kid—that my bicycle accident jump-started my depression as a teenager. I became so irresponsible when I was drinking that when I got sober, I swung the other way. I had impossibly high standards for how I should act. And then I would rage when I didn't hit my imaginary mark. Goldman taught me to do less in my day. "Take your normal to-do list and cut it in half. Even then you'll be doing more than most people."

She taught me that my buttons were getting pushed not because I was doing too little but because I was doing too much.

When I got stressed, instead of feeling tired, I would feel hyper. It felt like an avalanche was coming toward me, and instead of stepping to the side and getting out of its way, I would try to outrun it. I became bossy. I organized people. I felt like I had superpowers and could rise above it all. But there was always a price to pay for that pretense. A few days later, I'd go into a full-blown rage.

I wasn't a person who could process her feelings in the now; I had about a four-day turnaround before I knew I had feelings and what they even were. Some people have fight-or-flight responses. I have a frozen one. I freeze, then I fawn. So many eff words, so little time. So many feelings and no way to access them. Even today when people ask me how I feel, I often say, "I am not sure. Talk to me in four days."

Goldman began showing me how anger gave me a false sense of power. Feeling all-powerful was another way of dissociating. Slowly, she taught me a way to allow, access and then navigate those feelings. She gave me basic instruction on how to take care of my emotional life. Basic things like: drink water when I am thirsty, sleep when I am tired, and pee when I need to pee.

She agreed that all parents shape their kids' lives, but she didn't ascribe to the idea that it was all my mother's fault. "What a terrible narrative!" She felt it was society's bias toward blaming women: that hating the mother was a form of sexism so that no matter what a woman did, she could never get it right. Again, she blamed Freud. "Freud! The same guy who said women had penis envy. The only time women have penis envy is when they see their paycheque."

Oh, Dr. Goldman, you made a joke.

I was more honest with her than anyone before her, but I was still selective in what I revealed. I only brought up the topic of God once. I never mentioned Ruth's witchy sessions, because I was protective of Ruth and didn't want Goldman to dismiss her as some whack job. When I got too ethereal or spoke about my

Higher Power working things out for me, Goldman's eyes glazed over. Privately, she may have prayed and begged God like everyone else, but she seemed to think it had no place in therapy.

She showed me how to have boundaries through the way she ran her therapy business. She was a cultural Jew. She kept the Sabbath. Occasionally, she had to cancel if someone died because she had to sit Shiva.

In that, she showed me how to value my time. Human beings are constrained by time. If we don't treat time with reverence, it will take control of us. For someone who had no respect for time, who spilled time like wine running down the side of a cup, this was a tremendous gift.

But most importantly, she taught me how to end things. David and I had decided to leave the city, and I told her I wouldn't be coming anymore. She asked me for a debriefing session. To have closure. I hated the word *closure*, because when I have tried to tie things up with someone in the past, it has usually ended with screaming and slamming doors. But with Goldman, I saw the value of ending things skillfully.

It was a skill I used, years later, to end my marriage and say goodbye to my brother.

Then, we were done. Dr. Goldman ended the way she began: "Is there anything more I should know?" I took a second.

"Why did you lift your butt cheek during my sessions? Was it because I was going on too long about things?"

And she said, "No, I have a lot of patients, and I get uncomfortable sitting all day."

"Okay, okay. For two years, I thought you were passing gas."

And for the first time, Dr. Goldman laughed. Once she started, she couldn't stop. Apparently, Goldman was no better than the rest of us and loved a good fart joke.

Then she said this: "Ha! *Koved.*" Which is Hebrew for respect.

BARDOS

1. gap, interval, intermediate state, transitional process, or in between and usually refers to the gap between lives.

THE HELL HOLES

I **hunted down the fecking Irishman** like I was in the IRA. His
name was Ryan (or Bryan, depending on whether he was talking to me in Canada or to his folks back in the old country), and he
had a reputation for treating women like dirt which meant I was
drawn to him like a moth to a flame.

I met him a year after my divorce. Despite the fact no one
worked harder than we did to make our marriage work, it didn't.
And despite knowing that, for a couple of years prior, I was still
afraid to let go. I didn't want to be one of those fifty-year-old-
women living in a basement apartment with no windows. But the
day I said it was over, I didn't care if I was subterranean.

For the first while I didn't think about men. But at the one-year
mark, it was as if I had been following the divorce handbook: lose
weight, get a water bra, and go to town to get me a man.

On our first date, he took me to see the Dalai Lama. Go big or
go home. I didn't understand a word the Dalai said because Ryan
had that new car smell. Leather interior, all the bells and whistles.
He was so hot, the smoke alarm had gone off, and we hadn't even
started cooking. Who knew the Dalai Lama's talk on world peace

could act as a kind of foreplay? But it did. Some people eat oysters, but a man of faith is my aphrodisiac.

I was trying to take it slow, which is still double the speed of most people. I kept us busy. The ballet. The opera. Anything to avoid sex. On the fourth date, he drove down from Toronto, and I had organized a brisk fall walk to the Hell Holes to keep us focused on getting to know each other.

The Hell Holes are about ten miles north of where I grew up and have a series of underground caves, aptly named because to climb in and out of them is hell. But in the fall, they are beautiful: one hundred acres are carpeted in orange and red leaves. We paid our admission and were a few yards into the park when we came upon two people copulating. The woman was bent over a tree, ass in the air. The man had his pants down around his knees, pumping her madly from behind.

"Holy shit," I said, and the woman turned around and said, "Oh, holy shit,'" and then hopped into the woods with her pants around her knees as the man hopped after her.

My family thinks these things happen to me because I am a comic. "Leave it to you," they sigh. Like I was the one with my ass in the air in the woods. Or that I conjured this up. But it did happen. If I had come upon this scene with a friend of mine, we would have laughed about this for hours. But it left me incensed. The whole point of a brisk hike was to avoid sex and not witness a live-action tutorial. The Fecking Irishman thought it was a hoot. He couldn't quit laughing. The more he laughed, the more prudish I became.

"That is not funny." *Yes, I decide what is funny. I work for the comedy police.*

"You're a comic. Don't you have a sense of humour?"

Telling a comic what they should and shouldn't find funny makes us furious. And don't tell us what joke we should put in our sets. Even if it's brilliant we won't use it just on principle.

I trucked over the hill and dale like I was being tested for my hiking badge. As I raced through that forest, the short Irish Fecker and his pasty white Gaelic peasant legs couldn't keep up.

He yelled after me, "Slow the feck down!"

Going at quite the clip and yammering a mile a minute, I began a breezy commentary on the Hell Holes' history, which now sounded like a dirty metaphor after what we had just witnessed.

We then went to town for a quick bite, and he left for home. When he called me that night, he said, "You folks do things differently down in the country."

By then, I had recovered some decorum, "Well, they are the Hell Holes. They act out the seven deadly sins, and the first installation was lust."

Lust was what was on the menu for me, too. This was the first man I had wanted to sleep with after a twenty-year marriage. I may have been extraordinarily promiscuous in my drinking days, but now as a single fifty-year-old woman, I didn't know what to do.

Or what I wanted.

Or how to do any of it.

Friends said to just enjoy it. But try as I might, I couldn't go back to twenty-year-old energy. My twenty-year-old self always sacrificed safety for excitement. *Let's get naked and then see if you are a serial killer or not.*

The Fecking Irishman was suave, devastatingly attractive and contrived. Dangerous for me. After the affair was over, I saw that everything he did and said sounded like a movie script. But in the middle of it, I was so rattled by him that it took about seventy-two hours after every date to figure out what I felt—and that feeling was usually insulted. Three days later, often, a creepy sensation would come over me. I would feel sick to my stomach, remembering something he said or did to undermine me. Despite his sophisticated veneer, he was a crass man. He took me to the symphony and then walked me out of the theatre and said he'd booked a room at the Holiday Inn. I went along with it. He'd take me to a restaurant in Yorkville and order only the best food, then bring me home for sex and send me packing into the night. He appalled me, but I kept going back for more.

One night he brought God into the conservation. He said he had prayed a lot about us, but when I agreed and said I prayed too, he turned on me. "I will let you know when God wants us to take the relationship to the next level." I didn't know what irked me more: that he was praying about us so early in our relationship or that *his* God trumped mine.

Every single part of me was screaming: *Run, Deb. Don't walk away, run!* but I was running on pure cortisol, and I kept going back one more time.

Does that smell like shit?

Yep, it does!

Let's do it again.

Sleeping with the Fecking Irishman was like crawling under an electric fence. I didn't know when I was going to get zapped.

Lust, the sin I loved the most in my twenties, was now doing me in. The first relationship you have right after a divorce is a lot like making pancakes. You need to throw the first one away. Because even if this guy had been the nicest man in history, there was desperation in me. I was in the middle of menopause, at the mercy of hormones that were surging and waning. My friend who studies Kundalini yoga said women have a surge of energy before their V-Jay goes dormant. My vagina was having a going-out-of-business sale.

I "broke up" with the Irishman by phone, but when I told him it was best we didn't see each other anymore, he told me he wouldn't accept my decision.

"I will call you later," he said.

Six hours later he called. I didn't pick up. He left a message informing me that I couldn't break up with him because he was breaking up with me. Even in your fifties, dating is still like in Grade Nine.

Withdrawing from this guy was worse than getting off of cigarettes. I was craving him.

What do you do when you are withdrawing from a Fecking Irishman? Go online dating. Dating sites are the real hell holes.

I needed a man, but I was stingy. I didn't want to pay for one, so I went on Plenty of Fish. I had never dated online and likes and swipes didn't work for a codependent person like me. I'd write and rewrite a reply, and then when they didn't respond, I'd be devastated. And if we agreed to meet, it was terrifying to go out on a date with people I didn't know. But to even call these "dates" was a misnomer: they were more like meet and greets. Drivebys.

It seemed no one liked the idea of getting to know you. Some wanted relationship security before we had even had a coffee. Others had wild views of sex that were out of my comfort zone. Call me old fashioned, but I think we should find out each other's last names before engaging in performance art. It was like putting on a Fringe show: you work really hard, and nobody comes.

Yes, another joke.

Finally, after a few months, I got off the dating sites because I knew my time of chasing men was over. If one came along and it happened organically, fine, but I was not going hunting anymore.

Ruth, the crone from Casa Loma, warned me of this. "One day, you will walk into a room, and you will not turn any heads." I thought this was the saddest thing I had ever heard.

Then it happened. One day I walked into a room, sat down, and realized that no man looked at me. It wasn't as sad as I thought it would be because I realized I wasn't looking at them either. It felt odd, like when you think you've lost your glasses and they are on top of your head.

This didn't mean I wasn't able to love. Instead of rescuing a man, I rescued a dog—Gus. The shelter had shaved his back end because he had fleas. When I saw him, I thought our haircuts were the same.

If I didn't know how to be single, Gus didn't know how to be a dog. He didn't understand the word *leash*. Or *walk*. Or *sit*. He didn't do anything but sit on my lap and sleep. But he and I walked the South Shore. And while I wrote plays and comedies in my secret place, I hugged him and whispered, "I am going to get you fixed, so you won't hump people's legs when they come to visit, because if Mommy's not gettin' any, neither are you!"

David and I are still friends. We have spent eighteen of twenty of the last Christmases together. I helped him with every move. He let me stay at his house when Kevin was ill. We have kept our promise to love each other 'till death do us part.

We just don't do it under the same roof.

137 I LOVE YOUS

We weren't the kind of family who said "I love you" willy-nilly. Not unless you were in a coma or a coffin—we got lovey-dovey after you died. The men on my dad's side were kind, loving men, but after you turned thirteen they never made eye contact with you. On my mom's side, you were relieved if some of those uncles didn't see you at all. They turned every physical contact into something dirty. We didn't hug when we said goodbye. A firm handshake was fraught with meaning and a pat on the back was as close as it got to falling apart. We were Irish, so we had generations of stuffing it down behind us.

In my early twenties, a distant relative went on a walking tour in France and when she came back, "I love you" began to show up in family conversations. Because I longed to be more European, I began to say "I love you" when I left my parents' house. The first time I spit out those three words, I remember it felt like time stopped. They stood there slack-jawed. Then someone broke the silence: "Well, I'll get you to the train then," and it seemed the clock on the wall began to tick again. It was no easier for me. I'd start thinking about how to get this exit line out about an hour before I was set to leave.

We kept at it until, eventually, my mother said it back. It seemed like something she had been waiting for her whole life. Dad never did get comfortable with it. When I said, "I love you, Dad," he kept the *Napanee Beaver* in front of his face.

My mother would poke him and say: "Put that paper down, Jim, and say I love you to your daughter. That's what they do in the city."

And he'd mumble, "I love ya."

"Love *ya*," never "Love *you*." He couldn't commit to that extra vowel. The statement was quickly followed up with a "Do you need money?" It was never easy for us. But my kids came along and they said it as freely as we said hello or goodbye. It flew out of their mouths like soap bubbles. My son said he loved me so often, I began to think there was something wrong with him. He told me later he had to say it even if he didn't mean it because of Ned Flanders—from *The Simpsons*. Ned's wife, Maud, had died— apparently out of the blue—and Ned hadn't said he loved her that morning and would not forgive himself for at least an entire epi-sode. My son didn't want to end up like Ned Flanders, so he said it every time he left the room.

One morning, I snuck those three words into the end of the phone conversation—with Kevin. I said, "I love you."

"Well, I don't feel very comfortable with that."

"I don't care if it makes you feel uncomfortable. I'm saying I love you whether you like it or not." I made it sound like a threat.

Then one night, after many weeks, I heard a frail voice say "I love you" back. The floodgates opened and we couldn't stop. We became like two teenagers on the phone: "I love you." "No, I love *you*." "You hang up." "No, *you* hang up."

During that time, we said 137 I love yous. *Yes, I counted.* When people said that what we were going through was hard and that it was terrible, I begged them not to feel bad for us. I didn't want their sympathy. Yes, it was tragic, but there was also something important happening to us. We both had let down our guard because he was dying. Without death pending, we would have stayed stuck. We never would have woken up.

During that time, it felt like we were connected to our root system that went back decades, even generations. While Kevin's tumour was invading his left brain, we were using the remaining cells to connect the dots of our lives. We were sure we could see the big picture. Not like God saw, per se. But more like a satellite circling the globe, like Google Earth, snapping photographs of the intersections and avenues of the past. We could see our lives mapped out with a new perspective. See things we had never noticed before. Like this: Kevin was born two months after my mom's best friend, Erma, had died. He was their firstborn son; he should have been a reason for rejoicing, but they were too worn out to be happy.

Erma died of a brain tumour. *That must mean something.*

"Did Kevin catch that tumour from Erma?" my mother asked during one of the drives back from Ottawa. "Did I give it to him, somehow?" Mom asked this a hundred times when Kevin was dying. *Of course not, Mom. Of course not.* It was an asinine thought, especially since Erma died fifty years before. But Kevin and I were running with this kind of logic too.

Less than ten years after Erma died, I fell off my bike in front of Erma's old house, and years later, Kevin got a brain tumour. *Isn't that weird? Doesn't that mean something?* Did my life change irrevocably when I hurt my head? Is that when my attraction to people having brains that worked off-centre started? Were the downtrodden and broken sent to me as low-flying angels to accompany me whenever I travelled over rocky terrain?

After our visits, I'd return home looking for the plenty in every nook and corner. I appreciated the shit out of every day. I walked down the street and connected with people as I walked by. Out of the blue, people began telling me about their lives. The man in my building showed me how he planted trees while the rest of us slept. Drunks came up and told me they couldn't stop drinking and asked me to point out the nearest AA meeting. Rich women with yappy dogs told me about their suicidal husbands.

Even Preacherman seemed better. One day I was in the convenience store and there was a petite man ahead of me in line and from the back I saw knife marks in his head. Even before seeing the Repent sign on the side of his head, I recognized the voice. He was wearing the same luxurious coat and scarf, but his eyes were different—not haunted but soft, compassionate—and he was shorter than I remembered. Barely five feet tall. No wonder he needed a box to stand on. He turned around again and said, "Hey, do I know you?" I didn't say anything, and he continued, "I am Bob."

Bob. So that's his name.

"Hey, Bob. I'm Deborah." He smiled, and I smiled back. *Was he saying hi because he remembered me watching him? But nothing on his face said this was registering with him.*

I bet he wasn't religious at all. It was a mental-health crisis. *What happened to his other identity? Preacherman disappeared because he was back on his meds or off them.*

As Bob left the store, he turned back to me. "Keep it real, eh?" If Preacherman could change, who knows what miracles could happen?

PURGATORY

The crisis that drove Kevin into the hospital that final time was hiccupping for ten days straight. It was excruciating to watch his diminished body convulse. After he was admitted to the hospital, the priest was called yet again and after the last rites, Kevin rallied, again and again and again.

In the movies, deathbeds look noble. Dying people make their peace and say some loving things to their friends and family then drift off into the sunset. In real life, people linger. The ones sitting vigil get exhausted and become upset at the wrong things.

After Dad died, I had taken a hospice course. I wanted to be able to know what to do to show up for the dying better. At the end of his life, we missed so many opportunities to connect because the disease was all we became fixated on. I wanted a better way of navigating loss.

The first night, the course facilitator had us each tell the room a little bit about ourselves. Personal support worker. Nurse. Pharmaceutical rep. When it came to me, comic. People were taken aback, but I thought that the journey from comedian to hospice made perfect sense.

I thought it would be depressing, but after a night of talking about dying, I felt energized. I couldn't sleep. It was life-affirming to spend time talking with a group of people who didn't shy away from a subject we were all going to face. Some nights we cried together and often we laughed quite hysterically and inappropriately. The more I spoke about my fears and apprehensions about my own death, the less the whole subject frightened me.

After the training, I did comedy shows to raise money for the hospice, then I got asked to teach the communication component of the same course. I called the segment "How to Talk to Sick People," and I offered tips and exercises I had learned in improv class on reflective listening and going with the flow. Soon after, I was invited to speak at palliative care conferences and was given a grant to produce a short film to educate people on how to use empathy when speaking to people on their deathbed. It was called *Walk a Mile in My Backless Gown*. Even with all my "look death straight in the eye" bravado, when Kevin was dying, I got lost in the reeds.

When it was just the two of us, chatting on the phone, or when we were at his cottage, I knew what to do. He wanted to be at the lake as long as he could, but he couldn't be left alone, as he had nothing in his head telling him certain things were dangerous. He had lost all his worry and the sight on the left side of his face. This meant he couldn't see people coming up beside him. He'd walk into things. Once he lit the gas stove and didn't notice his sweater had caught fire. Then he began falling.

During that last summer I would go on Wednesdays and feed him and make sure he got into bed for his afternoon nap. On one of these occasions, I was massaging peppermint oil into his heels, and we began to talk of the afterlife. Kevin had developed a theory that this Earth was purgatory. In the geography of Catholicism, there used to be heaven in the sky, hell in the ground, and in between was purgatory.

Kevin's thesis was: "Living on Earth is the real purgatory. Look at my life. This is the place where we work off all the pain we caused."

It was a kind of Catholic-Buddhist fusion.

Once he was admitted to the hospital, all the philosophical conversations ended for us. We were never alone. The days were long and boring, stuck in a hospital room, making small talk and asking each other inane questions. Why did Starbucks make their coffee so bitter? And what about the price of hospital parking? Can you believe how they ding you? Somebody should do something. I'm going to write to somebody. We should sue. Who were we going to sue? We were too hyper a family to ever sue. By the time we complained about something for a couple of hours, we would have lost our head of steam and end up doing nothing. We couldn't nurse a grudge long enough to show up for class actions and court dates. That would take too much focus.

As the days went on, we expanded our hatred to the entire hospital system, the Church, and the people who brought us casseroles. We can't eat one more President's Choice lasagna. How much money is that guy from President's Choice making from people with cancer? During one of our visits, we spent over an hour trying to figure out President's Choice's lasagna profit margins. There are twenty people on this wing with four wings to a floor and there are eighteen floors in this hospital so if only 50 percent of these people buy one lasagna per household during a two-year illness well that is ... a lot of lasagnas. Give me your phone; I need to use your calculator.

This line of conversation made me insane. I began doing math and researching the death process. I wanted to know what timeline we were working with. I found out there is a dying chart online that will tell you how close to death a person is. I don't know if the chart is meant for the dying person or the living. I can't imagine if you were gasping for your last breath, you'd be googling such a thing. It is graded one to five. One is life. Five is death. I checked these numbers every day. I didn't want him to die, that was the opposite of what I wanted. But this was no quality of life so I just wanted to know how much longer I could plan to feel this bad.

God might laugh when you make plans, but he really howls when you try to figure out when someone is going to die.

Kevin hovered between a 3.5 and a 4 for weeks. No matter how much we all begged the power that runs the universe to release him from this mortal coil, the death dial didn't budge. He wasn't following the death chart protocols and a part of me was furious that he was lingering. *This is just like him. He never had a sense of timing. He never knew when to end the story and get off the stage.*

I was completely selfish but I remember thinking: I come from a big family and if everyone in our brood was going to take this long to die, I was going to be stuck in a hospital or a funeral home for the rest of my life.

Conversely, I felt a deep connection to my brothers and sisters. I was proud of how our family showed up for him. All of us had a complex relationship with Kevin and yet we never stopped going to see him. Somebody was either driving him to an appointment, helping his kids, or doing something to keep his life running as smoothly as it could. When somebody got tired, we tapped that one out and another one of us took over. It was not planned, it just worked out that way.

While in the hospital, we circled the wagons to protect him from outsiders. Well-meaning people who'd show up unannounced at the hospital, some distant relatives who dropped by to say hello.

"Who are you again?"

"I knew your dad. I was married to his second cousin."

They meant well, but all of us wanted to scream: "You never visited him when he was healthy. Why would you want to come now? Did you come to gawk to take the news back to your family?"

We were entering the homestretch. We didn't want strangers to witness his drooping to the side and his ubiquitous hunger. Steroids made it so nothing satiated his appetite. We'd take whipped cream and shoot it into his mouth. He looked like a bird grasping at worms. He never stopped eating and swearing. Kevin always had a potty mouth and loved filthy jokes, but now he was singing one off-colour ditty over and over again—something Grandpa had taught us as kids: "Here I sit broken-hearted, paid a dime and only farted." It was stuck on repeat. I glared at him, trying to get him to shut up.

"Okay sour puss, it's a joke," he laughed, starting up the second verse again.

"It's not funny," I said. I know I should have laughed it off, but this song sickened me. I'm a writer and since his days were numbered, I wanted him to say something more profound. Not just for my sake but for the sake of those around the bed, listening.

He was such an intelligent man, who, during many of our phone calls, shared with me so many great words of wisdom. How about the line about religious people: "We shouldn't be worried about getting into heaven. We should be worried about getting people out of hell."

Or when things were rough and I would be upset about something that he was going through: "These are just the moments of our lives."

Any of those thoughts would have been a perfect last line for people to remember him by, and if he didn't want to use his own, he could've borrowed Dad's famous last line.

As they wheeled my father out of the house for the last time, he turned back to us and winked, "The old tomcat is going out tonight." That would've been a great line to go out on. A line like that was quick and clever. If anyone accused Kevin of plagiarizing, he could have said he was paying homage to our father. Two birds, one stone.

All of us were running on empty. Kevin's family in particular. My dear mother was one raw nerve. Nobody could soothe her. If people in her community dared ask her how Kevin was, she'd fume: "What the hell do they mean by that? He's not dead yet. Those SOBs already have him in the grave." If they didn't ask about him, she'd be equally offended. "They are complete and utter ignoramuses, pretending they don't know my son is sick."

She prayed incessantly. She often went to Mass during the week, but now she snuck in late and left early because if she lingered, some well-meaning parishioner would hug her. "Why the hell are they hugging me? The only time I want people hugging me is if I have a gristle stuck in my throat and they're giving me the Heimlich maneuver." Sometimes she drove to Mass in the next town over, so she could pray in peace.

Every single day she was praying for a miracle, and when it didn't happen, she prayed all the harder. One part of me hated that she thought this was going to save him, and the other part hoped she was right.

What I wanted was for her to put down the rosary beads and offer us comfort. For once in her life, to rally the troops and lead the family in this final battle. "Why can't she be a leader for once?" I remember saying this one day. What was I thinking? There wasn't some Tony Robbins hidden in the recesses of her being that she hadn't let out yet. This was her at her best.

Her grief always trumped ours. When Dad died, it was: "You don't know what it was like losing a husband." With Kevin: "You don't know what it is like losing a son." Without knowing it, we had qualified for the Olympics of suffering, and no matter how hard we tried, she was going to win the gold. Plus, she was eighty-five years old, having to face the death of her son. It was all backward and she was barely hanging on.

We all regressed to our childhood roles. We were obsessed with talking about every move she made. She was the one whom we took our cues from. If she was okay, we were okay.

On summer nights in our childhood, after she went to bed, the little kids would go down to the basement to my sister's bedroom and mine. I was working by then, so I'd order pizza (a really big spender) and we'd talk about what our mother was thinking that day. Nothing had to have occurred for us to do that. We always had the pulse on her moods. Now, nearly fifty years later, we were doing the same thing. What was her emotional temperature? Is she running hot today? Is she giving the cold shoulder? Then we began dragging out old injustices from the past. We grazed on a buffet of old hurts with the emotional bandwidth of thirteen-year-olds.

As satisfying as character assassination can be, it left a bitter aftertaste. I'd made huge inroads with my mother over the years, and I'd go and sully it all by slagging on her. Maybe gossip is how families bond—how we prove we have a commonality. But after our trashing-mother sessions, I would feel sick. After all the work I'd done on myself, I should have been better than this, but instead, I three-wheeled on the backroads of bitchiness.

Kevin, now half blind, began proselytizing: "Guys, she can't give something she doesn't have." Months before, this would have been a profound statement we would have thought was the wisdom of a dying man, but now we were just annoyed with him. What the hell was he talking about? He was looking for something she didn't have to give, just as much as the rest of us.

As the tumour ripped pieces of him away, it was her he cried out for. "Mom, I want Mom." We tried to mother him, give him things he never got from her, but every time someone got in the car to drive to Ottawa, he'd say, "Bring Mom." Mom wanted to be with him too, because when he'd call, she'd drop everything she was doing and get her duds on and go. She'd make sandwiches, buy cheese (she always brought him a brick of mild cheddar cheese) and wrap the rosary beads tight around her hand and go to him as fast as somebody's car would take her. My mother showed up. She always showed up for us. No one could take that away from her.

I believe she, like all mothers, wanted to make it right with the child that challenged her the most. But when they got together, she and Kevin got stuck in the same old familiar loop. She'd end up babbling about inane things no one cared about. "Cheese was on sale and so I bought three pounds and kept one pound out and froze the rest. Did you know frozen cheese tastes no different than regular cheese?" I remember praying, *Please put this conversation out of its misery.* Kevin didn't want to hear about frozen cheese any more than the rest of us did.

One day, my mother and I were in the room alone with him. He'd dropped the fart joke and began to swear at her. "Fuck off with your cheese bullshit." Fuck. There was no word she hated more. She'd give long dissertations on the overuse of the eff word in this generation. "Why do people need to say that eff word every time you turn around? There are other eff words you know? Faith, family, fun."

In my world, I said the eff word so often I sounded like a flock of geese on a pond. But when I was around her, I always managed to censor myself. I took great pride in not saying that word in front of her, even when I was in seventeen hours of back-breaking labour with my son. I did list all the musicians I dated in the '80s, but I never said the eff word.

When Kevin swore at her, she turned to him and said, "You know I don't like that language."

Kevin hurled another eff-bomb at her chest: "Fuck you."

I think my heart may have stopped. Grab the paddles stat. Time slowed down like it does when people die in a TV Western. She had been shot through the front of her chest. "Why don't we all have a nice scone?" I asked. Over the previous two years, I had kept the scone place in business, buying dozens of them to feed people who weren't hungry. *Starve a cold, feed a tumour, isn't it?* My eff words were "feed folks flour."

"Mom, the caramel scones are to die for." *They'd go perfectly with that frozen cheese.* Maybe if our mouths were full, we could get this train back on track.

The two of them wanted connection, but instead, they lobbed insults at each other like they always did and when they ran out of ammunition, they'd turn to the person standing next to them and start in on them. That day the person was me. Kevin turned to me and slurred, "Deb. Go ahead and tell Mom what you said to me. Tell her how you had to go to therapy for years. Tell her all about how you are still screwed up by her."

"Kevin, I am not ..." I had told Kevin about the Goldman sessions in confidence.

"Well, what she thinks of me, that's her problem." Mom was now speaking to Kevin like I wasn't standing right there.

"Lard? Does anybody want some lard?" I offered my mother the box, and she pushed it away.

"I get kind of sick of my kids judging me."

Judging her? I was trying to help her. I wanted to go see Kevin alone. Have one last visit. But everyone insisted she come with me.

I drove down from Toronto and arrived at her house too early, so she wouldn't speak to me for most of the trip because she had to finish saying her rosary.

"Mom, please stop," I said. I was furious but I was smiling a huge Cheshire grin. The smile that I gave people in my St. Clair West neighbourhood had morphed into the smile of someone who had had one too many Botox shots.

221

Kevin kept pushing, "Mom, you gave her three fucking pens with no ink. What was *that* about?"

Mom turned around and snarked at me, "What pens?"

"Nothing, Mom. We're good." After two years of Goldman's sessions, I had put the pens issue to rest. I had created boundaries about what to expect and what to do around her. I knew where she ended and I began.

Then she said, "You write, don't you? I figured you could use a pen."

At the speed of light, without dropping the smile, without even as much as a breath or a pause, I hissed, "But why the hell would I want pens with *no ink*?"

"How would I know the pen didn't have ink?"

"Pens. It wasn't just one pen with no ink; you gave me three pens that didn't write."

"Well, your father always bought garbage. Besides, do you even use pens? You most likely write your stories on the computer." We were getting nowhere with this line of questioning. She wasn't going to get off the hook this easily, so I changed tactics.

"What about the beer-bottle opener? Why did you give me a bottle opener?"

She said, "Why would I give you a beer-bottle opener? You don't drink."

"I know I don't drink." I feel ashamed of what happened next. I still had the beer-bottle opener in my purse. I had carried it around even when I changed purses over the years. I don't know why. The mystery of the three pens and the beer-bottle opener had been resurrected.

I shook that beer-bottle opener at her and a smug smile came over her face.

"Excuse *me* for caring about you," she said. "I know you like to drink your Diet Coke from a bottle, so I thought you could use it."

She was lying and she knew I knew she was lying. Kevin was laughing his head off. *What is so funny? You started this whole mess.* No. I was above this. I wasn't going to get mad. I had learned to respond to her, not to react to her. I leaned in to hug her and she bristled, then she changed her mind, moved toward me, and then I changed my mind and walked away from her.

At this point, I remember myself gesturing to the hospital room door and miming an exit, "I am going to ... well, I will ... will let you two have some time alone together." As I was leaving the room, I almost knocked over a cleaning guy, who was entering the room pushing a mop.

I walked quickly down the hall, feeling like I might split in half. Trying to find a place where you can let out a primal scream is impossible on a cancer ward. The place is in constant motion. There is no place to catch your breath, let alone bawl your eyes out. The halls are crawling with nurses and support staff coming and going. Patients and their families whispering and comforting each other. Inside each room, there is one person after another lying in bed, many looking far worse off than Kevin did.

The land of the hungry ghosts. Haunted people looking out from their rooms, waiting for the Grim Reaper to come in and take them away. As tears rolled down my face, I caught the gaze of a man lying on a gurney, gaunt, gray with raccoon eyes who, when he saw me, fixed my gaze and cried out, "I want to go home!" I smiled and held his gaze for a minute. *I know you do, buddy. Don't we all?*

WHAT IS
THE UNIVERSE
TRYING TO
TEACH YOU?

When some people get exhausted and run on empty, they go to the gas station and fill up the tank, but not me. When the indicator says fifty kilometres to empty, I think the car is lying to me. I see how much farther I can push it until I run out of gas.

Kevin had been given the last rites in September and it was now December. And it seemed this wasn't ever going to end. He was just going to hover between life and death indefinitely. I was in no mood for the holidays and yet again I was on the road, thinking this would be the last time I'd see him. And this time, it was.

I picked up my sisters in Napanee and we drove to Ottawa. But when we arrived, tensions were high and a squabble ensued— things were said that couldn't be unsaid. I was not involved but I witnessed it and since we all came in the car together we all had to leave together. We went up the elevator to see him, and after a five-hour drive to get there, six minutes later we were in the car going back home.

I dropped my sisters off in Napanee and picked up Gus, then I decided to go home to Toronto by way of the Sandbanks. I needed to be by the water and find some peace. I went to the abandoned beach. In the summer it would have been jam-packed with umbrellas and beer and tanning bodies. But it was empty and completely blanketed in snow. The dog and I walked for nearly an hour in the bright sun that forced me to take off my coat; my face was red with sun and wind burn. A great lake is a place to ponder the deeper things of life, and on this cold, bright winter day, it did not disappoint.

As I gazed out at the water, Gus was tucked inside my coat, staring out with his underbite jutting out. My breath and the heaving ice breaking up beneath the surface were the only two sounds I could hear.

By the time I got back in the car, I felt almost human again. I knew I had to stop rushing everywhere. It didn't matter how long it took to drive back to Toronto, I would just take my time. I meandered down the provincial road to get to the main highway, cranking "The Race is On" by George Jones and singing as loud as I could in the key of off. Kevin and I had listened to George Jones and sang the song in the middle of the night when I walked him to the bathroom—a song sung so neither of us would be embarrassed by such a personal act.

He'd sing it so often it became an ear worm that played on an endless loop in my brain. I remember begging him to get off that tune and onto something else.

"What other songs do you want them to play at the funeral?"

He shook his head. "I don't know. I haven't thought of any other tunes."

Everyone should keep their funeral music selections up to date. Picking something like "The Locomotion" by Little Eva is cute if you have a tragic death at fifteen. Or Meat Loaf's "Two Out of Three Ain't Bad" might be funny while you are still partying, but as you mature, you eventually see it's a selfish choice.

Because your funeral, much like a wedding, has nothing to do with you. You must think about how to create a mood for those who showed up to pay respect. You must set the mood for how you want them to feel about your life. Think of your selections more as a soundscape of your life. An emotional piece, then something sacred and, if you must, something slightly upbeat and humorous, so people will say, "What a card she was."

"We've got to work on your music choices."

As this memory flooded my mind, I realized I wasn't going to go back there for one more visit. I was done. I do something until I don't, and then I move on. I pulled up to the stop sign just outside town and became lost in thought. I accidentally let my foot off the brake and hit the car in front of me. I was sure it was only a light tap, but before I knew it a nice woman got out of her vehicle and said she better call her husband, and then there was a policewoman pulling up beside me. At this point, I was still thinking we were just three women who had each other's backs in a Sisterhood of the Travelling Pants sort of way. But then the woman in the dinged car drove off and I was told to stay behind because the cop said she must charge me. Reckless driving.

"I hate to have to do this, but what can I do?"

My brother is dying, lady. And I'm never going to see him again. So maybe you could let me off, you silly cow, that's what you could do.

Because I was running on empty and I didn't want to beg this woman for mercy, I ended up apologizing to her for making her day harder. That's what I do when I am furious. Apologize. As she issued me a $400 ticket that had me lose six points, I said sorry. She softened and said, "Don't worry, you can take it to court and fight it." *Or you could just not give me the ticket in the first place you twit.*

As I pulled back onto the highway, I thought this day couldn't get much worse. I was wrong. There is no quota on how many garbage things can happen to one person in one day.

About an hour outside of Toronto, I realized I had missed my pit stop and needed to pee. It was rush hour and the westbound traffic had slowed down to a crawl. I inched along at ten kilometres an hour, trying to remember how to do Kegels. I was having a hard time holding on. I looked at Gus sitting next to me in the car. *He'd be absorbent. But no. That would be wrong.*

I began reciting repeatedly in my head, *I am not going to pee my pants. I am not going to pee my pants. My bladder will not defeat me. I have survived a divorce, a premature baby and teen-agers. I can do this. I can control my bladder.*

I yelled at my smartphone, "Siri! Where is the nearest coffee shop?!"

"Sorry, I do not understand." *Of course not.*

In the rearview mirror, I saw a turkey roasting pan in the back seat. It was still there from Thanksgiving, but as I put my arm over the seat, trying to grab it, it was beyond my reach. "Siri, throw the roasting pan into the front."

Siri shot back, "I do not understand."

You do understand, Siri, but you are just being miserable. Would it not be useful if Siri could throw me the items I needed? Now *that* would be a smartphone.

My exit was five hundred metres ahead.

I gripped the steering wheel and slowly edged onto the off-ramp. There was a Harvey's sign flashing up ahead and with clenched buttocks and teeth, I sang their theme song: "It's a beautiful thing." I was going to make it. *Nope. Nope. I am not going to make it.*

Traffic wouldn't allow me to get even close to the hamburger joint, so I was forced to pull over on a side street. I got out of the car, covered myself with my coat, then pulled down my pants and placed the turkey pan in its proper place underneath my haunches.

There was a slow, gentle rain. Oh, a soft, heavenly, Leonard Cohen "Hallelujah" kind of rain. It was the worst and best thing all at once.

Suddenly, a horrible thing happened. The angle of my dangle wasn't quite right. When I was younger, I was like an assault rifle.

Now, I was like a sawed-off shotgun. It was spraying everywhere. I was going to have to detail my car.

Eventually, when I got back to my apartment, I called my friend and told her about my day. And she said, "Next time ..."

"Next time?" I cut her off. "There isn't going to be a 'next time.'" Did she think I was going to make a habit of peeing my pants?

"Next time, fold up a diaper and put it in the glove compartment."

"I think you are missing the point. Everything is just going so wrong."

To which she replied, "What do you think the universe is trying to teach you?"

The universe is trying to teach me not to call you. Of course, that great comeback came to me hours after I hung up.

What *was* the universe trying to teach me?

Two years of trying to be a good sister to Kevin, trying to wring out every drop of meaning from our relationship, all the time knowing the whole thing was a losing proposition. And how did I get rewarded? I lost six points off my licence, wet my pants, and, worst of all, after getting kicked out of that hospital room, I knew that was the last time I was ever going to see my brother alive again.

I don't think the universe is trying to teach me a goddamn thing.

KOANS

When I went to the Buddhist temple it was snowing.

There was a new sensei—a woman who loved reciting kaons. Kaons are a riddle or puzzle that Zen Buddhists use to meditate upon. Zen masters have been testing their students with these stories, questions or phrases for centuries. It's a Buddhist form of a Rubik's Cube. Or mind-fuckery.

They don't make sense, but this one takes the cake: A young man and a young woman from warring families in a small village fell in love. Knowing they'd never be allowed to marry, the boy said to the girl, "Meet me at the dock after sunset and we will escape from our families and be together." That night, under the moonlight, he waited for her, and when she arrived, they paddled to the nearest village to make their life together.

Within months she became pregnant, and they decided that their families couldn't continue to hate their union with a new grandchild on the way. They paddled back to their village, and when they got to the dock, the young man said, "You wait here. I think it will be safer for me to go tell your mother and father first. Once the coast is clear I will come back and get you."

The young man knocked. When the girl's father opened the door, the father began to weep. "Thank God you've come. Ever since you left my daughter has been asleep in a coma." The young man was bewildered. As he entered the bedroom, he saw his beloved sleeping in her childhood bed, and like all tales like this, he bent over and kissed her. As she woke up, she said, "I've been dreaming about you." Which story was true? Was she with him the whole time, or was he just a part of her dream?

That's a kaon for you. It's a classic *what the hell* moment.

A ten-minute discussion ensued with some of the tall thinkers, the brainiacs who wanted to discuss this conundrum instead of just watching our breath like we normally did. The whole thing made my brain feel like a ball of wool after the cat got at it. Sensei asked us to return to sitting Zazen (sitting on the pillow) and think about what the kaon meant.

For monks, this is entertainment. A great puzzler for noodling on in a Korean monastery up in the mountains. When you take vows of austerity and celibacy, what else do you have to do with your day?

I hated those two lovers and their parallel universe.

As everyone was watching their breath in those sub-Arctic temperatures of the Zen temple, trying to figure out what that dang kaon meant, I sat cross-legged on the frayed, thin pillow, realizing that Kevin had been my kaon. A puzzle I had wrestled with for two years.

In one universe, I had made a living amends to him. In the parallel universe, nothing had changed at all. I was broken, physically, emotionally and financially, and wondering if any of the love I felt had happened at all.

I began sobbing, wiping mucus away with my sleeve, and all the while those bone-thin ectomorphs sat there with their eyes cast down, looking a few feet ahead of them, not moving a muscle.

I felt like my brain might burst into flames. But if it had, the buckets of tears I was shedding would've put out the fire.

Someone hit the gong, and I slowly got up and bowed to the plastic Buddha statue, put on my shoes and left. For good. *No, Kevin, I am not a Buddhist. Was I ever one?* Sure, it helped break me free from my rigid Catholic upbringing, and I will always use some of the ideas. But like many people, I had thought anything Eastern was exemplary, more pure and exotic than Christianity. But it had many of the same flaws and blind spots.

As I walked out onto the street, I saw the building next to the temple was now a daycare. I remembered the days when it used to be a Baptist church. In those days, I would watch all those big, beautiful women waltz up the church steps with their brightly coloured dresses, teetering on high heels—so high that wearing them could give you a nosebleed. Black and caramel-skinned women with fascinators the size of sunflowers growing out the side of their heads. If I closed my eyes I could see them inside the church, swaying and singing "Down in the River to Pray." I thought to myself I should've been a Baptist. If you were crying in their house, they would've had the decency to offer you a Kleenex.

A COMIC WALKS INTO A MOSQUE

People said it must have been hard to perform with so much going on, but doing comedy was the one place I felt good about myself.

I had been booked at the Kingston Islamic Centre and was quite worried that I wasn't the right performer for a mosque. I had performed many gigs for groups I didn't know were religious until it was too late. Once, at a gig, I sat down at the table with some of the members of the audience, put my napkin on my lap, and someone asked if I was the comic. Just the way they spat out the word *comic*, I knew enough to lie.

Female comics were and still are a threat to many people. If men make a joke people don't like, they brush it off, but women tell a bad joke and people treat you like you committed a war crime.

"No. Not a comic," I said. "I'm more of a motivational humourist."

"Good, because last year that girl comic was too dirty, and we threw buns at her."

"Buns?"

"Yes, because we're good Christians."

I wasn't sure what part of the Bible dictates throwing buns at people, but I did know that usually when someone starts a conversation with the words, "I'm a good Christian," chances are they aren't. After that statement, I got on stage and mentally began cutting every joke that I thought might offend them. Every time someone reached for a butter knife, my body involuntarily began to twitch.

Now, in the Islamic Centre, I felt like an ignorant small-town girl. Growing up in Canada in the '60s, I didn't know any Muslims. I didn't even know any people of colour. In my town, people of Italian and Portuguese descent were as pigmented as it got. Of course, when I moved to Toronto in the early '80s, my mind opened to many more cultures and religions. I went to a synagogue with a friend to explore Judaism. I bowed to the goddess Devi at the Hindu temple. But I didn't know a thing about Muslim culture, and I was worried I would put my foot in my mouth.

When I expressed my concern to the woman from the mosque's Muslim Women's Steering Committee, who was hiring me, she said she saw it differently. "You're female, and they are female. Plus, funny is funny."

I prepped as best I could and got there early to case the joint. I do this before a performance because it calms my nerves. When I went to the washroom, the first thing I noticed was a surprising tool in each stall: a watering can. I had no idea what they were for. When I returned to the main room, women had begun filing in. Most were wearing a hijab. There were black hijabs that framed the face and hijabs with brightly coloured designs. One lady wore a burqa that covered her from head to toe, with only a small screen in front of her eyes.

I kicked off the day by admitting my limitations. This was a trick I learned from Larry King on CNN: Be honest with the audience. Tell them upfront what you don't know. I walked to the front of the room and said, "Let me get this off my chest. I just went to the bathroom. I don't know what the watering cans are for. Was I supposed to do some gardening while I was there?"

Laughter erupted. Even the woman in the burqa was laughing—or I assume she was—her shoulders were moving up and down. They yelled out that watering cans were a rudimentary bidet. After relieving yourself, you swish some water in the under regions. They began mocking its usefulness and even poking and laughing at each other. *I was going to be okay.*

Fifteen minutes into the talk, the woman who hired me signalled it was time they took a break. The cheese trays and the chocolate fountain rolled out. It was 9:45 a.m. I couldn't start eating chocolate at 9:45 in the morning—I'd end up in a diabetic coma by lunchtime. I went to the bathroom and used the watering can and when I came out, I looked like I had wet my pants. Again, I said so in my set—more laughter. I countered with "Next question. What does the chocolate fountain symbolize?" The woman in the burqa stood up and said, "It symbolizes that we like chocolate."

"Maybe you'd like to be up here?" I asked, and she walked partway to the stage to join me. She was killing it.

After lunch, a local physician spoke, then it was my turn again. On the surface, it might look like a lapsed Catholic from Napanee might not share a lot of history with Muslim women who, I had learned, hailed from around the globe, but I knew we had something important in common: women who came before us.

"To understand who we are as women," I said, "We need to look back to the moments before this one. Back to the women in our lives who shaped us, and where they came from. Can you imagine your moms and grandmothers having the things you have today?" Heads began nodding. "My grandmothers Kimmett and Brady led very different lives from each other. They were rural women. Always home, always sitting on their couches. They sat there just waiting for us to visit. We'd drop by and then stand in the doorway for ten minutes telling them all the reasons why we couldn't stay. They were very different kinds of women. Grandma Brady wore her wig in a darkened living room. The drapes were always closed because the furniture and her face would fade if they were exposed to light. She'd light up a smoke. She'd give me one." One woman in the back shook her head disapprovingly. "I was the only eight-year-old I knew with smoker's fingers." Then another woman in the front nodded.

"When the priest asked Grandma Brady, 'How's it going, Mary?' she'd say, 'I have ten kids. It's going all the time, Father.' Grandma Kimmett didn't talk sass like that. She just sat there delivering a long stream of consciousness about long-dead people from time periods we never lived in. Grandpa sat at the end of the couch. Grandma Kimmett was heavier than him, so he was just a little bit higher. And one time, while Grandma Kimmett was talking, Grandpa fell off the armless couch, which left Grandma sitting on a bit of a slant. She looked like she was sitting on a half-cocked ironing board. Was he drunk? Had he had a stroke? No one ever said. Especially not Grandma. There he was, lying on the floor, and she kept on talking and we sat there doing nothing. It was like she had us in a trance. When he finally got up, Grandma Kimmett, without missing a beat, said, 'You had a nap did you, Vernie?' If Grandma *Brady's* husband had fallen on the floor, she'd have taken her lit cigarette from her mouth and flicked her ashes on him and said, 'Have you been into the rye, old man?'"

I now saw almost everyone was hanging off every word, so I took a deep breath and continued. "We can laugh at our grandmothers, but if your grandmothers are like mine, they had little schooling, no agency over their bodies and no opportunity to pursue their dreams. And it was they who laid the foundation on which we were to build our lives."

Even with the jokes, I was always so kind to my grandmothers when I spoke about them, unlike when I spoke about my mother.

Why was that? I didn't want this to be my story anymore. If I couldn't be nice to her in person, I decided, I could try being kind on stage. I started way back at the beginning. "As a young girl, my mom was happy; there are pictures to prove it. There is a black-and-white picture of her as a fat baby in a big bowl sitting in the sun. Pictures of her as a teenager in her bathing suit, kicking up her legs. There are stories about her dancing on the table when her mother and dad went to town. But by the time I was born, it seemed that all the humour had been sucked from her bones. All her memories were painted over with blood and gristle. It was the harshness that many children of the Great Depression faced. From a young age, she was taught if you weren't working like a dog, you weren't working. Those were lean times and they taught Mom to be frugal—so much so that she would put her gum in a spot inside the kitchen cupboard so she could chew it later. She'd take one stick of Wrigley's and divide it between the six kids."

A woman in the front row looked over at an older woman—who I thought might be her mother—and poked her in the ribs. I continued my speech.

"Mom reheated her meatballs until they were so dry we could've used them as hockey pucks."

Stop with the jokes, Kimmett. For once, let her be a hero in the story.

"She was no longer poor—but a humble beginning never leaves you. If you complimented her, she'd slap it away the way you'd slap away a man with a stray hand. Turn even a compliment into an insult. I am a lot like her. For all my self-improvement I too believe every act of kindness will be immediately followed by another shoe dropping." This made me choke up. In a room full of strangers, I could be vulnerable, but when I was with her I was defensive.

I soldiered on with my speech.

"My mother, like all women of her time, always made sacrifices. When she got married, she gave up her career. She didn't use birth control because that was what the Church commanded. She had six kids. She always said that's how many she wanted. But what else could she say? She lived in a day when that was what society and the Church had laid out for her." I paused and took a breath. "Even though I know her life was harder than mine, why do I still secretly believe I am better than her?

"Didn't she want a life better than what was laid out for her? Just like me. My mother wanted education so badly after her sixth child was born, she went back to school. It took nine years of night courses to get her B.A. And she graduated from university the same month I graduated from community college."

Applause erupted, which was less about my performance than about respect for my mother's journey.

"That feat was huge, and in fact she ended up going back to teach school, finally getting the financial independence she longed for." I felt a cry coming on. The back of my throat tightened, but I imagined my voice overriding the tears—above the wave of emotion. It was an acting technique Marie had taught me, but I overcorrected and the voice went up so high it was almost a falsetto. Think Minnie Mouse meets helium balloon.

"I had so many more chances than she did. Yet, I spent most of my life trying to get her to approve of my dreams. Often I gave her authority over my happiness. She was the barometer for how well I was doing."

My mother was not God. I had heard that from the priest in Regina years ago. Now, in front of these women I didn't know, I truly understood I was still making her a deity. Didn't my mother want the same thing from me? For me to look at her and say 'Mom, you did good.' To adore her even a little like I did as a child.

Water rained down my cheeks. One salty tear landed on my lips, and as I licked it off, I heard my mouth make a strange creaking noise. The same creaking noise my mother made when she was trying to stuff her feelings down. *Not only did I look like her, now I had the same strange noise leaking from my body.* I sounded like a plane coming apart in mid-air.

"Aren't we all searching for a perfect mother, who can give us perfect, unwavering approval? A mother who doesn't exist in real life." I had to gain control of myself before I crashed into the side of the mountain. I made some smart-ass comments about needing to get an oil change and then ended with a "we-are-women-hear-us-roar" platitude and sat down to crickets—complete silence. So much for my big finish. Maybe "they" were wrong, maybe honesty isn't always the best policy.

After what seemed like an eternity, the woman in the burqa stood up and hooted and hollered, and fifty women followed suit. Our cultural locations might have been different, but the emotions were universal. Women came up to me and, while giving me hold-on-for-dear-life bear hugs, one after another, they whispered fragments of their stories in my ears.

Many had moved across the world to find a home where they could blossom. Others had earned multiple degrees and learned several languages while pushing up against racism and bigotry from the outside world and strict codes within their families. Sometimes the moves they made were something they reached for, but many times, it was something they did for survival. But the commonality was we all had a mother.

I soaked up their love, their hugs and accolades which didn't just feel good, it energized me. Forget koans. Human connection was the way to go. As I let go of a hug, the woman in the burqa passed by and hip-checked me, "Maybe I should be a comedian, eh?"

"Maybe you should! You really should."

WHIRLING DERVISHES

"It was long before,** in the time when the buffalo ran freely across the Earth."

The woman at the front of the room blew the words of a Kenyan poet into the microphone. Wild Moroccan music pounded. The wooden dance floor beneath my feet seemed to bounce. It was Wednesday—Ecstatic Dance Night at the Dovercourt House on Bloor.

Ecstatic dance is an ancient form of movement that people of many cultures use to access the divine and, in the weeks leading up to Kevin's death, it became a sanctuary for me. When the hall vibrated with music from around the world, mixed by a DJ from Bali and influenced by Sufi and Indigenous cultures, I couldn't hear myself think. The beat began slowly to limber up our bodies and spirits. Coming in off the street, where I'd been putting out fires, it was hard to encourage my body to move freely, but the DJ, with a voice halfway between shaman and dominatrix commanded us to land our feet solidly on the floor: "Now we feel the earth beneath the soles of our feet, let us ground ourselves into the here and now."

We were a gaggle of misfits, college students and some old hippies moving independently, wildly, across the floor. They called it a safe space. No alcohol consumption. No dancing with people without their permission. And best of all, no talking.

Newcomers like me always try to circumvent this rule. Whenever someone tried to air-whisper one of the dance guides came over to them and put a finger to their lips. The best part was I knew no one. I never took friends there because they wouldn't have behaved. They would have made jokes and so would I. I went with my daughter once and we couldn't make eye contact or we'd collapse into fits of laughter. As strange as this environment was, it was freeing to be anonymous. I stopped censoring my every step. Self-consciousness slipped away because this was a place where, whether a person could dance or not was not the point. Neither was what you looked like. Some people had dancers' bodies. But many, like me, were flabby and scarred with stretch marks with flushed red skin.

Awkward movements and arm circles, moving freely in our various sizes and genders: Ecstatic dance was the one night when my concern over what I looked like left me. I put self-hate on pause and slid across the varnished floors with unbridled joy.

The place was full of wild hot bodies and mine was one of them. The music gathered steam. The DJ belted out her next instruction: "Move deep into the bowels of the Earth and imagine dancing with your ancestors."

I couldn't imagine my ancestors in this space. My people are a bunch of wankers and horse thieves. It would be scary to call forth my forefathers from wherever they might be hanging out. Besides, most of them couldn't dance. Especially the men on my dad's side, who don't move from the waist down. At dances, they would be outside drinking with their friends by the truck. Oh, maybe if they got drunk enough and some woman complimented them enough, they would get up on the dance floor and never let go of their beer.

They'd stand there bleary-eyed, holding their ale with a stupid smile on their face as they bounced up and down like they were pumping the well for water. Imagining them there, watching from the sidelines, made me smile. What would they make of these free forms with their bare bellies and bindis, doing contact improv dance, bending backward and laying on top of each other's bodies as if they were benches?

My great-grandfather worked in a quarry and rolled rocks up hills using his back. My ancestors worked till their backs broke, so, on their days off, they sat there living from the neck up.

I pounded my bare feet into the hardwood floor, and I could feel my body get rid of months of stress. I was soaking wet. We are a dry people who don't sweat even after the gym, but my back was soaked. Perhaps it was the heat or the music, but suddenly I saw my brother lying in his hospital bed in Ottawa. His breathing was shallow. I saw in my mind's eye a tornado funnel of wind about two feet above him. His hands hung loose along the railing of the hospital bed. My head was pounding. The buffalo music drummed on, and then an image of a white snake comes up through my feet. My back arched as it passed through my body and slithered off into the night. Suddenly, violently and without warning, I ran to the bathroom and threw up.

The next morning, I was teaching the last week of my online writing class. I was teaching them that in good storytelling, the ending is in the beginning—the question you asked at the top of the story has to be answered in some way by the end. Right on cue, my brother Vernon texted, "It's over." No all caps, no exclamation points. Two years after he was told he had a year to live, Kevin was dead.

AFTERLIFE

THE PRAYER OF
THE SCONE

"You need to start** honouring your grief," Rachel said. I had known her for decades, and she was a person I could call when I needed someone who would give it to me straight. She was unfazed by anything you told her. If I had called her and said I killed somebody she'd have been right over with some bleach. But when she told me to honour my grief, it pissed me off. I wanted to say my grief didn't honour me. It had no respect for my plans for the day: It got up ahead of me in the morning and was sitting at the end of the bed smoking a Gitanes cigarette when I woke up. I'd come to crying with my arms outstretched like I was an infant reaching for its mother. Even though I had made it right with Kevin, my grief was not handing out hero cookies or hugs.

For years, I had never needed an alarm, as my internal clock went off as the sun rose, but without the daily calls to or from Kevin, I woke up later and later. When I did finally get moving, I felt like I was walking through quicksand. Coffee. Gratitude for coffee. Walk ten-thousand steps. Appreciation for legs that could walk to the scone place by 11 a.m. and be back watching Netflix by noon.

If you could keep your grief focused on the dead person, it would be easier, but you don't wail and gnash your teeth and cry out their name every day. No, it doesn't work like that. Grief zigs and zags and screams at the wrong person. When it finishes with the outside world, it attacks every good thing you've ever done in your life. While you sleep, it seems to compile a litany of memories of every other grief you've ever had: your childhood dog, Mittens, that got hit by a school bus; all the times you didn't get the job you wanted, the job you had tried to attract. And what about your Grade Five boyfriend, Scott, who said he'd drive you around on his lawnmower then dumped you for your best friend, Roberta? Let's do a roll call on all the times men have disappointed me.

One memory that replayed every morning for close to a month was of my dad, crouched over the bed, dying of lung cancer, while I played Louise Hay's CD *You Can Heal Your Life*. Cringe-worthy memories that you can do nothing about and have little to do with the grief on hand.

It was February when Kevin died, and it didn't help my mood that Toronto was a sea of grey. It seemed the neighbourhood changed hues overnight. I could see St. Clair West for what it was: flat, ugly and gentrified. If I had lived in the desert, a tumbleweed would have blown by on cue, but I was in Toronto so only reused plastic grocery bags blew out of the recycling bins, littering the streets like limp condoms.

Then there were the magical moments between the people in the building who bothered to talk to me. Helen, with the towel on her head, stopped chatting to me and started telling other people in their building that their faces weren't wrinkled either. It was her go-to line, I guess. Marlene was sober now and walked into her apartment without so much as a "hello."

I didn't need the likes of them anyway. I began putting earplugs in, listening to podcasts with Ricky Gervais and Russell Brand battling it out about the existence of God. Russell in his predictable manic way, a guy you'd never be able to win an argument with, saw a mysterious multi-dimensional, multi-universal connection in everything. Ricky, on the other hand, thought the connection was not proof that there was any mysterious entity running the place, but this fantasy we had about God was more an evolutionary mechanism to find meaning. Ricky's clever brain confirmed that there was no God and Russell's hyperkinetic mind went off in all directions trying to prove there was.

Why couldn't I be an atheist like Ricky Gervais? He's hilarious and far more successful than me. And he's not walking around praying. When he's analyzing the shit out of humanity, he's making a skillion dollars doing it.

I wanted to be like Ricky, or even like my friend Randy.

Randy was a good guy. A sensitive, feminist atheist, an environmentalist and consumer of only plant-based food. And he sent texts with prayer hands with evergreen tree emojis. *What do those evergreen trees mean anyway?*

In 2017, God was no longer trending, so it was the perfect time to lose all faith. Atheism was to 2017 as Buddhism was to 1970. People were denigrating religion. It was time for the patriarchy to be crushed and as for the Catholic Church, it was taking one hit after another. Sex abuse scandals, and then the discovery of the mass horror of residential schools. It was endless and heartbreaking. I am sure Jesus was looking down at the Catholic Church during this time and thinking, "Leave my name out of this."

Over the years, I had created a patchwork Higher Power that worked for me, but looking for the good in everything suddenly felt like bullshit. I was sick of looking for lessons and meaning. I was no longer deconstructing organized religion or deciding what pronoun to use for the divine after Kevin died. I lost access to something within myself that I had created to give me comfort. I didn't believe in any mysterious force. I felt I was back to the person I was standing on the subway platform westbound on the

Bloor line, not able to go back to my old life or move forward with a new one. This didn't just create a dilemma on a personal level, it also created a problem for the many alcoholic women who I was helping in recovery rooms. Women I'd convinced that there *was* a Higher Power, something divine that cared that they lived. After talking them into a god, wouldn't it be bad form to go back to them now and tell them that I had stopped believing in anything?

Most of the time, I didn't even know their last names. Some told me that they loved me, bought me windchimes and made mixtapes of Indian throat-singers chanting the Bhagavad Gita, but most of them didn't offer me as much as a thank you. Most of these addicts were so arrogant, they thought they were doing me a favour by telling me their woes.

So yes, I was sick of hearing about their bad relationships and their self-inflicted wounds. I didn't need that. I was not a therapist. Or their mother. I was not Marie Hopps either. I would often imitate Marie. I'd even use her lines. "Take your hand off the bouncing ball," I would say. But I was never going to be Marie. I was not ever going to be some peaceful older woman because I don't like tea. I take a cup once in a while when someone offers but I don't like it. I can't grow a long, grey-haired braid like she did because my hair is too wild and unruly. I don't have a British accent and I can't eat plain digestive cookies. I only eat the ones with chocolate on one side, and when I start, I can't stop. I eat a whole sleeve, and then a box, and before you know it, I am ordering a gross from the cookie factory. How can I ever become a wise old lady sitting on a chair if I have no control over my cookie consumption?

Find someone else to tell your petty little troubles to, to be your guru. I am having a crisis of faith.

I told the recovery women I had been helping that I needed a time-out. I needed self-care. (Self-care: two of the most overused words when you are grieving. How many hot baths can a person with psoriasis take?)

On the outside, I still looked good. In public, I answered "How are you doing after your brother's death, Deb?" with "Fine. Excellent." Big mouth, loud laugh.

I was still spouting off all of my classic Kimmettisms, like "When the monkeys are circling the airport, don't clear them for landing." That was a favourite of mine.

"There are no spiritual airmiles; you don't get a toaster for being a good person."

"Dust yourself off with a feather, not an SOS pad or brillo pad."

Keep the worried people at bay with one-liners.

I didn't just hate my grief. I hated other people's grief as well. When friends on Facebook posted that one of their relatives had died, I clicked on the comfort emoji and said I was sending love and light, but I wasn't doing anything for their dead relatives. I had enough dead relatives of my own I didn't pray for. I didn't care about their family, nor did I believe that me sending them love or light did a bit of damn good.

The scales had fallen from my eyes. When my Aunty D became a Charismatic Catholic—which is the crystal meth level of Catholicism—she told everyone the scales had fallen from her eyes. She actually believed scales fell from her eyes. That Jesus had given her a spiritual eye lift that meant she could see not only what was right for her, but for all her kids and everyone she met.

Now I was taking a page out of Aunty D's playbook. Seeing how it is is a lonely proposition. It's alienating to be mad at everything, to be poking holes in anything anybody says, but I didn't care because I didn't want most people around me. I wanted those do-gooders with their pathetic faces and casseroles to go home and leave me alone. Only a handful of people know what to say when someone dies. I knew this from Dad's death. Often people say dumb things like "he's in a better place," or worse yet, some act like nobody has died. They say nothing at all. They tell you some petty story of theirs, like how they are saving money for a car but then the taxman dinged them.

I regressed to bingeing.

When I first moved to St. Clair and Bathurst, I had a scone a day four times a week. After Kevin died, I bought five a day. I didn't even share a morsel with Gus. *Don't give me that look, mister.* I didn't bother taking them out of the bag, just reached in and broke off chunks as I walked back from the scone place, gnawing at little pieces and holding them in my cheeks like a squirrel until they dissolved into a paste.

Pieces dropped onto my shirt and down my bra, and one night I thought I had a lump on my breast, but no, it was just scone crumbs. Tiny scone cysts.

Sugar has always been like heroin to me. I'd binge like crazy on it then I'd go to the methadone food. Salty, crunchy, fatty things. All the O's. Cheetos, Fritos, Pork Rinds. Deep-fried fat. Fat fried in fat. I ate fried butter. I thought it would either kill me or knock some sense into me. It didn't because this wasn't like booze. No matter how big my ass got, it didn't make me stop. It seemed my big ass was never going to hit bottom.

By the time I called Rachel, I was bingeing morning, noon and night, not knowing how to stop and not sure if I even wanted to. "I made amends and I did the right thing by Kevin, and now my life is a complete mess. He is dead. I am broke," I began.

My whole reason for coming back to Toronto was for more work, but at that time I couldn't get arrested. Financially, things were so bad a friend was threatening to start a GoFundMe campaign for me.

"You need to pray," Rachel said.

"I might be an atheist. I've been talking to Randy."

"Randy? Randy? Randy talks more about God than any Christian I know. I call him a born-again atheist." She wasn't wrong. For someone who didn't believe in God, Randy sure went on about it in every conversation.

"It's just that I'm so mad at ... God," I said.

"Let me get this straight: You're mad at this God that you don't believe in?"

Don't confuse me with my own words.

"Whatever you call it, you need to connect to your inner wisdom."

"What if I have no inner wisdom, ever think of that," I responded. I was having an old-fashioned temper tantrum.

"Because you're eating your feelings." Rachel took a long breath. "You're stuck in your head."

Yes, I was stuck in my head. I loved my head. My biggest desire was to be a brain in a jar, talking to other brains in jars.

"You need to get down on your knees and pray," she said.

"What? Why? It hasn't come to that."

I got down on my knees a few times in my sobriety, off and on, but part of rebuilding my faith was not doing what I had been forced to do as a child. I was just fine sitting on a couch, or walking on the beach, and the God, Internal Peace and or whatever the hell name I was giving it this week, didn't require any knee work from me. I hadn't prayed on my knees in years.

"I'll light a candle or buy some essential oil, but I'm not kneeling over some scone made of lard and currants."

"It's not just lard and currants." Rachel continued. "You always think it's just the lard and currants. It is you disconnecting from your body when your body needs you most. It's been this way with you for a long time now."

Over my life, I'd gained and lost dozens of pounds. I had paid thousands of dollars to stop eating—Weight Watchers and TOPS. I'd been sugar-free, gluten-free and carb-free. I counted my points.

251

I tried intuitive eating. "Eat a butter tart every afternoon, mind-fully." Mindfully? One tart and I would want a dump truck full of butter tarts and then begin bingeing and having to put my coat on over my pajamas to make another trip to the store. When I stayed overnight at people's houses and they told me to "help myself," they had no idea what they were in for. I can't tell you how many times I have "helped myself" and had to wake up early to go out to shop to replace the food I gorged on in the middle of the night. Despite all that, I never took my food addiction as seriously as I did my alcohol addiction.

Neither did other addicts. Or the medical establishment. Most professionals denied food's impact, thinking that a few PDFs of food plans would fix the problem. But deep down, I knew that when I started certain kinds of eating behaviours, I couldn't stop. Not because I was lazy or ignorant of the nutritional facts.

I remember telling Dr. Goldman about how food binges plagued me. I didn't come out and say it. I skirted the issue—"I wonder why so many fat people attend church. Ever think about that? God removes heroin addiction and the love of rum, but not so much the love of pie." I figured if I was going to have to do therapy twice a week I could multi-task and workshop my comedy bits. "I am not fat-shaming church people. I am just say-ing we never address the fact that maybe a person is eating so much because they don't know how to take care of themselves. We hand out prizes for women who take care of others but not themselves."

"What have these church people got to do with you?" Goldman looked at the clock, then she shifted her bum in the chair again.

"Well, I'm just saying there are many fat people in helping pro-fessions and religious circles."

"And ...?"

"I have a food addiction."

"I don't believe that food is an addiction," said Goldman.

Of course, she didn't. I pressed her to explain. "If it's not an addiction, why do I binge all the time?"

"You need to stop thinking of food as the enemy and start thinking of it at as a *mechaye*." *Mechaye* is a Yiddish word that describes pleasure—less a verb or a noun, and more of an experience. Eating delicious food is such a *mechaye*—a wonderful thing.

The way I ate food was rarely a *mechaye*. It was more a process addiction than a substance one, but for me it was just as devastating. Just like drinking, once I started eating certain foods, I didn't stop till they were gone. But at the time, I couldn't or wouldn't admit that to myself. I chose to believe her. It was better than doling out more cash for another pay and weigh.

"Rachel, praying on my knees doesn't work for me. It triggers me." Yes, I said trigger, one of the most overused and misused words of the time. The word *trigger* triggers me, but I went for it to get her off my back. "I find it pretty triggering that you are implying that my method of spirituality is not good enough."

"That's your go-to emotion, isn't it? To be offended?" she said.

Of course it was my go-to emotion. It was how I had made a very unstable living.

Before I could give her a sassy rebuttal, she snarked back, "You know, before you called, I was sitting here minding my own business. I didn't get up this morning looking to convince you of anything." She could work on improving her bedside manner. "You still have some big fight going on inside of you. Who are you mad at?"

Everybody.

Everything.

I was mad at things I hadn't been mad at in years.

At Kevin's funeral, I lay my head on the pew and sniffed it. As I did, a random thought came to me that Kevin and my cousin had varnished all the pews in the church in Napanee. It drew me back to him and the days when I had the faith of a child. Then I got in the Communion line again with that same level of defiance I'd had after my cousin's death by suicide decades before.

The priest said, "Now we will have Communion." Pause. "Just for the Catholics." Another pause: "All the *practicing* Catholics." If only the practicing Catholics had gone up to the front, about four people would have been able to receive the Eucharist. My Mom, Aunty D and her two other sisters.

Isn't the whole point of Communion to experience a connection to the love of divine Jesus? I didn't worship Jesus, or even call myself a Christian, but I liked Jesus. I had no bone to pick with his teachings. I walked up and dared the priest not to put the wafer in my hand. I placed it in my mouth and just like before, it got stuck to the roof of my mouth.

I was angry at the Catholic Church.

"I washed Kevin's feet, like I was Jesus himself. I even gave him a pedicure. That was a miracle, that we had gotten that far in our love. Of all the people in that church, I deserved Communion as much as anyone else," I said to Rachel.

"Of course you do, but you have nothing to prove anymore—to that Church, to your mom, or anyone. You took the Communion to seek approval from people you don't even like.

"I am pathetic."

"Not pathetic, as much as you are returning to what is familiar."

"And I am also mad because it all turned to rat shit."

"Darling, it always turns to rat shit when people die. Did you honestly think death was going to make all of you better people than you were when you walked in? Come on."

"Isn't that the point? To be better than when you walked in?"

"Here's the thing, Deb: when you came into sobriety, you had a lot to make right, a lot to be sorry for. But you've done that over and over again with your life. You can stop walking around looking for absolution."

I'm not asking for absolution. Why would she say I am asking for absolution? Yes, I did see the word repent tattooed on a guy's head on a street corner, and it set me off on a mission to repair damage done. Yes, it activated some kind of kinetic craziness that had me running back and forth from Ottawa to Toronto like a chicken with my head cut off.

In the beginning, I was doing okay. In fact, I had done a lot to take care of myself. But somewhere along the line, my own body's needs became secondary. *How could they not?* Kevin's disintegration was ubiquitous and brutal. Each week, he was losing ground, and with each new deficit, I barely had time to catch my breath. There was no rest, not one day where you could stop and say, "No cancer talk today." A day where you could just stop and show the Grim Reaper the hand and say, "Back the fuck up, man, we need a flipping minute here." No, the cancer kept coming for us.

"It's not that I didn't know what I was getting into. I walked in knowing we were going to lose the battle. I had accepted that."

"Oh honey, you may have accepted that he would die, but you did not accept that you ended up loving the guy, and it hurts like hell. You need to forgive yourself."

"For what?"

"For just being exhausted by the pain of this. It's okay to be defeated."

"That sucks."

"Yes it does. But start there. Pray to be guided back to yourself, back to your centre."

As desperate as I was for my crazy to end, I railed at what she was saying. "I can't get down on my knees, Rachel."

"It's up to you. Do what you like, and I will still love you."

I hate when people say it's up to me; it's an unfair tactical move. It takes the stuffing out of the fight.

255

"You pray on your knees?" I whimpered.

"Yes, I do. And I'm a Jew."

"Don't Jews pray on their knees? This is the first time I've heard of that!"

"Maybe you don't know everything eh, Deb?"

"I'm sick of begging."

She breathed in. "Praying has nothing to do with begging. Praying on your knees isn't that you lose and someone else wins. It is a gesture of humility. The body understands the shape of surrender."

Humility was a place I hadn't visited much in my life. It seemed interchangeable with humiliation. Someone lost. Someone won. When we hung up, I googled the word humility. *Humble* comes from the Latin word "humus." Of the Earth. Kneeling means I would be connected to Earth. I could do that.

I stood facing the bed. I looked down. It seemed like it was a long way to the floor. Why did I have to kneel anyway? Couldn't I get humility by standing up like a normal person? I placed my hands on the bed and bent my knees. I wondered if I'd get down there and not be able to hoist myself up again. What if I died down there? I'd be smelling up the building, and three days later I'd be found in the prayer position, Gus having eaten my face.

With about as much resistance as I felt in early sobriety, I bent down. One knee only. Wasn't that enough. *Pretend you are a footballer, taking a knee before the big game.* The second knee hit the hardwood so hard I thought I might have fractured something. I grabbed a feather hotel pillow I'd stolen from the Hilton when I was on tour years ago—oh to still be working. I stuck it under my knees and closed my eyes.

Closing my eyes, off in the distance I could hear the kids in the apartment next to me laughing, and their grandmother watching a Philippine soap opera. Gus lay down and sighed, wishing he'd been rescued by a normal person. I didn't swear. I didn't do an audition piece. For once in my life, I was too tired to do my normal song and dance. I didn't ask for anything. I didn't care if anything outside of me was listening or not. I put my hands together and lay my head on the side of the bed.

I had hoped my spiritual journey would have exorcized the Catholic out of me. But Catholicism is like addiction; you fight it one day at a time. You can't remove the parts of you that you don't like, because you'd lose all the parts that shaped you.

I was taken back to the church in Napanee. I could almost smell the high-gloss varnish of the pews and Grandma Brady's peppermint breath hitting my neck along with an array of one-liners. I imagined her begging me to come home with her after Mass. "Come back to the house and we'll have some butter tarts and a smoke." I could practically smell her cigarette breath and see her yellow fingers.

I had been arguing with myself for weeks, thinking I needed to understand the name of God before I asked for help again. It was still so hard for me to be humble and ask for help. Maybe I was afraid I wouldn't get it. So I stayed in my head, shadow boxing with my ego. I was a survivor. But after decades of debating, I was exhausted. I was tired of being consumed with trying.

I got up from my knees and crawled into bed. I woke up under the covers an hour later—afternoon nap drool running down my chin. Gus had his head on my stomach looking up at me. I felt different. Once again I needed something bigger than me to step in and help me. My body suddenly felt roomier and my shoulders had dropped. I still don't understand what it was, exactly, but it was the first day in a long time I went to sleep without bingeing.

I surrendered. But the feelings I had been avoiding were waiting for me.

Mornings were the messiest. I'd wake up crying. I thought about how I had gotten lost in the land of medical options. "This isn't a cure," they had said, over and over again, but we had hoped that somehow Kevin was the exception, that he would beat the odds.

When Kevin was alive, my heartbreak had some purpose. It grew compassion in me, and it brought me closer to him. After he died, my grief had nowhere to land. No wonder I used food to get a spiritual bypass.

Every day I woke up an atheist and then prayed on my knees for thirty seconds to a God I didn't believe in. But still I wanted to bully myself out of feeling my feelings because I thought what had happened to me wasn't that bad. My grief was not up to par.

My whole life, I've heard imaginary critics doing a play-by-play on my sincerity. When I meditated, I could hear some Born-Again Christians thinking I was going to hell. Dancing with the Sufis, I saw family members tut-tutting about what an oddball Debbie was. Even writing this book, I was sure I knew what my scientific friends were going to say: "What kind of person believes in God when science can prove everything?" Even Dr. Goldman came back to haunt me with some zingers: "You weren't window shopping for God, you were window shopping for yourself."

Writing an appreciation list felt like reaching for straws so I reframed it. It became more of a letter. I wrote to the divine as if we were having a conversation. Dear God. Sometimes I could use the three-letter word. On other days, I had such contempt for the three-letter word, I'd slip an extra o in and make the word *Good*.

Dear Good. Dear Ultimate Good.

The page has always been the place I could most be me. The place I didn't need to pose or shave off the parts of myself I found unworthy or too insignificant to mention. Instead of writing furiously, fearful my thoughts would vanish, now I would ask then pause and wait for answers. Waiting is hard for someone who always runs the light. Waiting required vulnerability. It required staying in the land of I don't know for a minute. Ten. Come in and sit a spell. It required making room for something quieter to enter the conversation. Graphic sensations would rise and fall in the body. Like junkyard dogs they snapped at the chain link fence. Other days they were puppies fetching well-marbled *bon mots* for my consideration. Mostly though, it was me, then the pen and the page writing my way back to myself.

Some days I couldn't sit and write at all. I would nearly crawl out of my skin. Those days I walked for miles and ate my face off. Despite that I began to forgive myself. No, *forgiveness* isn't the right word. It was: the more I stuck with myself, warts and all, the more I felt I could walk myself back to the living. I was hoping there would be a day when all of these parts of me would shut up and I'd be a spiritual giant; where I would be sitting on some cloud, filing my nails, directing traffic, above it all.

Spring, summer, sainthood.

Don't all people want that extra season?

GLORIOUS MYSTERY

I **wasn't looking for anything** but sun and friendship when I booked a flight to San Miguel de Allende. It's a desert town about four hours north of Mexico City by car. It was a couple of months after Kevin died and a couple of friends, expats from the States, offered me a stay at their casita, attached to their home. I needed spoiling, they said, some sun and culture, walking around the mountainous town.

It was weeks out from Easter Sunday, and Mexico had already begun its month-long Easter celebrations. Though most of Mexico is considered culturally Catholic, other pagan customs are also woven into the way they celebrate.

Mexico is shaped by sixty-eight Indigenous cultures, including the Chichimecas, near San Miguel, who inhabited that area thousands of years before colonization by the Spanish. The people were drawn to the region because of the many hot springs and, as a result, they built pyramids to honour the gods for their gifts of abundance.

When I took a walking tour of the pyramids outside the city, I was shocked that this small pyramid stood on a desolate land that we would consider a desert. With no visible water to be had, ancient Chichimecas managed to eke out a life in communion with nature, and because their lives were always on a dangerous precipice of drought and starvation, a lot of their practices involved ritual and human sacrifice to keep the gods on their side. After the Spanish invaded and decimated their way of life, forcing Catholicism down their throats, many people retained their customs in secret. This melding of faiths is called *syncretism*, which is defined as an amalgamation of different schools of thought. Interestingly, the Aztec religion was already syncretic before the Spanish invaded. Now, in modern times, Easter celebrations in San Miguel de Allende are a big spiritual soup. Part prayers and prostrations, and part non-alcoholic Jell-O shots, fireworks that go off every hour and balloon rides outside the church.

The Friday evening preceding Holy Week is dedicated to the Virgin of the Seven Sorrows. Throughout the town, altars sprang up and overnight vendors, in mule-drawn wagons, descended on the town selling clumps of wheat. These tiny sheaves of grain, combined with bitter oranges, gold foil and pictures of the Virgin Mary, decorate altars in windows and doorways of homes, and in the courtyards of businesses as throngs of people walk through the residential area. If I had been home in St. Clair West, where there is a melting pot of Portuguese, Brazilian and Cubans who celebrate Easter with parades and reenactments, I wouldn't have crossed the street for this dramatic display. I'd have written off this pilgrimage as old-timey Catholic and walked on by. But in Mexico, I walked through the streets, my phone lighting the way, as people invited passersby into their homes.

I was waved into one adobe. I bent down to avoid hitting my head on the low overhang of the doorway. Inside, a beautiful twenty-something woman with her hair done up in a scrunchy and wearing a blue razzle-dazzle shirt and rhinestone-studded pants, handed me a miniature cone cup—the kind my dentist gives me when she tells me to rinse my mouth. It was full of blue crushed ice resembling a slushy. "This is the Virgin's Tears," she said. Without a second of caution, I licked a concoction of blueberry ice cream with a hint of lavender. The Virgin's Tears were delicious.

My upbringing was Catholic Light compared to the Mexicans. On Good Friday, there was a live reenactment of Jesus's crucifixion. Crowds had quadrupled from the procession the week before, and people had come from all over Mexico and the globe. They were moving in unison, saying the rosary together—it sounded like locusts were about to descend.

Throngs of people made the long walk up the hill from Calvary, as actors began the reenactment. "Jesus" came into view carrying the cross on his back, and as the crowds parted, an older woman whispered to me that he was the best Jesus out there. I wanted to ask how she knew this, but I didn't have time as "Peter" came into sight, and Jesus shook his head in disappointment. "Peter, did you betray me?" Peter shook his head no. Violently. A little much, if you ask me. And then, just as in the Bible, a rooster crowed, not three times as in the origin story, but a good twenty times. Roosters crow all day long in Mexico, and if you can't hear a rooster crowing, a dog barking or a car backfiring, you aren't in Mexico.

The crowd played their parts. Some jeered at Peter, others yelled "Crucify him!" at Jesus. Instead of offering vinegar-drenched rags, some women offered Jesus sips from their plastic water bottles. Immediately, I was disappointed in them for not choosing a greener option. When "Jesus" sipped the liquid he was offered, I pursed my lips together and it felt like I had been quenched as well.

The unrelenting heat reminded me of the shrine I went to as a kid. But instead of a bunch of repressed white people with bad haircuts and A-line skirts, the people I was with were crying out for Jesus to end their suffering and getting the whole thing on their phones. A few crawled on their bloodied knees beside him. *Drama queens.*

At the top of the hill, Jesus lay down and was tied loosely to the cross. A man tied the ropes tighter and Jesus flinched. Some extras mimed pounding nails into his hands, and all I could think of was a thing Sue used to say to me whenever I was hard on myself. She'd take my hands and face the palms upward to the sky and say "No holes there. You're not Jesus yet."

This guy *was* Jesus, at least for the next hour. What kind of complex would that give a person? Playing Jesus every year? I saw he was wearing a wedding ring. That must be hard on his wife, being married to the town's best saviour. He was the Mick Jagger of Christianity. Every year, he'd likely start getting into character from Ash Wednesday onward. I could just hear the excuses: "I can't help with the kids. I am going to be betrayed in forty days." On Easter Thursday, he'd likely have to sleep in the spare room to get his head in the big game. I could see him there, rehearsing with the dog, practicing his famous line, "Hey Gus, should I say it like, 'Judas, was it YOU?' or 'JUDAS, was it you?'"

Fake Jesus cocked his head to the side, piously. I saw a fly buzzing around his left eye. He didn't flinch. No smile. No annoyance. Deadpan. He reminded me of the blackjack dealers in Jamaica or the King's Guard in bearskin hats outside Buckingham Palace. They had been trained not to react to drunk women trying to engage them in small talk. Even though I was not a drunk woman I still wanted to be the one to have him break character, even smile. I kept grinning at him like, "Hey buddy, I see that fly. Smile, damn it." A cloud passed overhead, blackening the sky, and right on cue, Jesus died. Following a few minutes of silence, a man with a white collar, packing a gun and a big belly, waddled toward the centre of the square. "Come back Sunday for the big finale." Then, as he peeled the foil off a Cadbury Creme egg that he'd pulled from his top shirt pocket, people began to disperse, and more big-bellied men let Jesus and the thieves down from their crosses. And replaced them with plastic mannequins—subs until the big event in the morning.

The same older woman who reviewed Jesus's acting said, "Will we see you then?" I smiled and nodded, but I had no plans to return for the sunrise hunt for the Lord.

I loved the Easter story even more than Christmas. It seemed to be the one story that honoured how much suffering humans go through in their lifetime. You don't have to be a practicing Christian to see that Jesus on a cross symbolized the crosses all humans have had to bear at times. An endless struggle where one minute you are a saviour and the next they want to stone you. A time when endless pain comes upon you and the three days (or three decades) when you are in the dark, you're waiting for the light to come back in your life. I wasn't looking for Jesus or anyone else to return. I think we give dead people far more credit than they deserve. Likely because none of them have ever come back to me.

On the morning of my dad's death, my sister said he appeared to her one final time. She saw his spirit fly from the hospital window. I was sitting right there when he died. I had been up all night waiting, and I didn't get so much as a goodbye or a kiss my arse. Maybe dead people don't visit me because I don't believe in them or the realms in which they are waiting around. I am not much into the afterlife—heaven, hell or reincarnation. I believed in reincarnation for a New York minute. But if you were not going to remember your past life, what was the point?

"How can you believe in nothing?" Kevin would ask me.

"I believe we live and die and that's that. I don't believe in any afterlife, which I think is very brave of me because I am nice to you for absolutely no good reason, Kevin." *Damn donkey.*

This is how I protect myself because I don't want to get my hopes up. I don't want to be walking toward the light crying out "Hey, is anybody home?"

Perhaps the biggest reason I wasn't going to get up on Easter Sunday at dawn was that I didn't want a resurrection. I didn't want to leave my cocoon of grief. There was safety there. Familiarity. I had built a fortress around myself where I could, for once, rest and take care of myself. I could still use my grief as an excuse to cancel plans with friends and not overwork, and I felt if I emerged too quickly, I'd get the bends. I'd be back to overdoing it.

The next morning, I woke up at 5 a.m., for some reason, with the aftertaste of a dream in my mouth. It was more of a replay of a real-life moment that happened between Kevin and me. He was in the Season of Endless Hiccups. I was sitting on the side of his bed, massaging his back, and no matter how many pillows I gave him, he could not get comfortable. Then he looked up at me and said, "I don't know why, but you always were so mad at me."

"Kevin, I'm sorry, really sorry, that I hit you with a frying pan."

"Well, I was likely being a pain in the ass."

"I'm sorry I picked on you. We all picked on you."

"Yes, well, but we picked on you, too. You were 'the weirdo.'"

My hands stopped rubbing his back and I laughed. "I think I was more of a leader."

"No, you were the weirdo. Those long stories you told that no one cared about."

"We were each other's weirdos." I laughed.

He laughed too and he reached his hand up to find me, for he was partially blind then, and between hiccups he said, "You've been terrific in all of this."

"Kevin, it's been my blessing," I said.

This memory had been smothered by the onslaught of early grief, but there it was in a dream in Mexico. I was strangely grateful that Kevin hadn't accepted that first apology I'd made to him. Because even though it was brutal being with him while he was dying I knew if I had the chance to do it over again I wouldn't do anything differently.

I jumped out of bed, climbed up the hill, and, as the sun rose, Jesus appeared out of nowhere, by a rock. He was surrounded by his groupies: Mary, Martha and the other Mary. One of the thieves was sitting there hungover with his family. As Jesus raised his arms to the sun, it was my life that flashed before me. I got a sense of my five-year-old self covered head-to-toe in psoriasis. The teenager self, when I was Debi with an *i*, who had a head injury, who wore that tragic wig to Grade Nine, who was so lost and afraid that she thought deep down she was evil. The hilarious young woman who gravitated into addiction, and that newly sober mother who had two children nine months apart, who was struggling to keep her head above water, then overcorrected and overcame and persevered.

When I walked back into the centre of town, a man outside the church offered me a ride over the town in a hot air balloon. "Want a ride, Abuela?" he asked. *Abuela* is Spanish for "Grandma." I am not a grandma. My kids only have cats. But I was too inspired to be insulted. I climbed into the balloon, and fireworks were going off in the distance. Fireworks go off all day and night on Easter Sunday in Mexico.

As we floated up above the city, it was the first time I knew that over my life I had indeed had many spiritual awakenings—independent of whether God exists or not.

That might not be resurrection, but it was close enough.

WINDOW SHOPPING FOR GOD

The last time I saw Preacherman, he was still yelling but he had changed up the script a bit. "Believe in one true God and ye shall know heaven."

I was sitting on my bench, drinking my coffee and peeling an orange. No scone from the scone place, just coffee—going to a scone place for just coffee is like going to a bar for a Diet Coke.

At the end of the month, I'd be moving in with my friends up in Richmond Hill. I needed time to get back on my feet financially and they had offered me a suite in the lower level of their townhouse. Low rent was one excuse, but after all I had been through, I needed to live with people. I needed connection.

Within weeks of moving there, the money would flow back in, and I'd be more creative than I'd been in years. I would write a play, get booked on some films and release my first comedy album. Gus would die and I would stop praying on my knees. Not being in a crisis, I would go back to walking and writing out my appreciation list.

Despite my worry that bad things always followed good, nothing bad happened to me. I didn't fall apart. I didn't binge. The committee of critics left me alone so I could sleep.

Before the move, I packed and decluttered everything from my apartment. I gave a lot of furniture to a young couple next to me who had just arrived from Brazil. I said an informal goodbye to the people in my building. Marlene was now clean and leaving at the end of the month as well—she'd got a job at a factory up on Bathurst Street. Helen's dementia had gotten worse, so the city had to forcibly remove her from her home for her safety. As gentle as they were with her, she cried like a baby, not knowing what she had done wrong or where she was going. The woman moving into my place after me was already having Amazon packages delivered. Megan Bowen was a shopper, it seemed. The world was moving forward—and so was I.

Bob had forgotten that he needed meds and was back to being Preacherman. Whenever I saw him, it struck me what a strange, magnificent organ the brain is—it houses two sides of the personality. One side is kind and generous. The other side is the lousy neighbour who keeps us up all night and tortures us with realities that don't exist. The only difference between him and me is he needed meds to pull the two off of each other.

Most of us believe we have control over these two separate realities. We think we are so autonomous and that sanity is a choice we make inside ourselves. But sanity is contingent on many outside forces. A dash of bad luck here, a chemical imbalance or a brain tumour there, determines whether the God we create is a loving parent or a ruthless taskmaster.

Preacherman's mind had him look through the lens of the harshest aspects of the Bible. Maybe that gave him certainty. The only time of the day he felt a sense of control. Although our stories were different on the outside, I wondered how I had not ended up like him. One more binge, a concussion, a more severe brain injury, maybe I would've been on a soapbox instead of a stage. We just had different outlets for the chaos in our heads.

He went into the Old Testament and I went into bookstores, keeping the self-help industry in business for decades, but none of those books were what I was looking for anymore. When I packed up to move, I gave the last of them to Marlene, and told her to skip to the last chapter where they tell you to love yourself. Those books were wonderful, but without someone helping me interpret the wise words inside of them, I would've been dead.

Without kindness from my fellow travellers, the wisest words would have fallen on hollow ground. Historically, it wasn't the wisest people who helped me the most—not the gurus or philosophers. Not the one-liners or exotic rituals to access the divine.

It was broken people. Usually, the most broken people of the lot helped reshape my vision of what the divine was. Danny, dying of AIDS, told me to believe in life not death. Marie said to take my hand off the bouncing ball, and those two men in the truck told me to show up for life. When I was broken in two, people would show up and reveal their brokenness with me, and that was when I felt the presence of God most.

For me, God needed skin.

For years, I felt my worst quality was that I could never settle into one spiritual practice. That I would get part way there and as soon as people wanted me to drink the Kool-Aid, I'd bolt. You couldn't make me do anything.

Playing the devil's advocate has been as much an asset as an impediment. For one, it's the key ingredient for being a comedian. Our job is to call out injustices, to be outside the window looking in, yelling out, "Hey, do you see what's going on in there?" That outsider view has shown me how similar things are from one spiritual practice to the next. Kwan Yin, the bodhisattva of Compassion, is similar to the all-loving presence of The Virgin

Mary. Norman Vincent Peale was old school; the law of attraction. This comparison was how I measured my progress.

I slip on the banana peel every once in a while. Just a while back, I found a course online in California called There's Nothing Wrong With You. When I told Rachel about it she said, "You're going to spend $1,000 to find out nothing is wrong with you? Let me do that for free."

I will always have a brain that thinks I need one more thing to be fixed before I am okay, but Preacherman had a brain that told him he needed the same thing day in and day out to feel good. He had only one script, one part of the Bible that he could rely on, day after day. Preach from 7 a.m. to 9 a.m. Eat breakfast. Come back and preach some more.

He was compelled to be predictable, and I was compelled not to be. I was an improviser and found it most exciting when I could hold two contradictory ideas inside of me as the Mexicans do. Syncretic Deb, they call me.

Take spirituality and science. They do not have to be ideas mutually exclusive of each other. What if the Big Bang Theory happened because God's head exploded six billion years ago, and all the particles from that brain made all living things, including: panda bears, mosquitoes, gnats, protons and quarks? Each of us, even me, got a piece of the celestial pie. Our job as humans, for the past six billion years, has been to be curious and try to connect so we could piece the brain of God back together.

A part of me wanted to share my philosophy with Bob. "Hey, Bob, remember when you yelled at me that first time not so long ago? Well, it did help me indirectly. Your yelling at me had me go back over my life. Then there was that time I saw the word 'Repent' on your scalp, remember that? Seeing that one word made me realize that I had no time to waste and my brother and I finally got to heal what had gone on between us. Bob, your particle changed my entire relationship with my brother."

But I kept quiet mainly because two different people were living inside of him and I wasn't sure Bob and Preacherman knew about each other. When he was Bob, we could exchange pleasantries—he was a man I could even see myself having coffee with. But when he was Preacherman, I am pretty sure he would've tried to turn my café latte into wine.

Maybe it was because I wanted to offer him some sage advice or maybe it was because I was leaving and would likely never be yelled at by him again, but I walked over to his soapbox and said, softly, "I know you're trying to help people, but doesn't that yelling hurt your voice?"

He looked down at me like this was the first time we met, and then responded in a way that I still think I made up. "Should I modulate my voice?"

Did he actually say that, or was I wandering off into fantasy land again? Before I had time to figure it out, he continued, "My counsellor says I should speak softer. That I'd get more flies with honey than vinegar."

I wanted to say you'd get more flies with bullshit, but I didn't want to get him riled up again.

"Try lowering your register," I offered, and he leaned in and pushed his ear forward as if that would make him hear me better, and he nodded his head as I talked: "If you lower your voice, it might have more impact."

There I was on a street corner giving Preacherman acting notes. For a brief second, neither one of us was afraid of the other. It seemed the whole world vanished into the background, as we had a brief moment of connection. If you were a passerby you'd think we were just two performers sharing ideas on how to hone our craft.

ACKNOWLEDGEMENTS

D &M publisher Anna Comfort O'Keeffe for choosing this book, Caroline Skelton for being a boss at editing, cover designer Heidi Berton, production intern Colleen Bidner, and Luke Inglis and Corina Eberle in marketing and publicity.

Special thanks to early readers: Susan Alexander, Sue Reynolds, Debbie Innes, Janet Munroe, and Laurel Brady (daughter) who read and edited several drafts.

The cheerleaders: Celia McBride, Catherine Dorton, Lesley Krueger, Urjo Kareda, Len Whalen, Pat McNichols, and Carol Redmond.

The mentors: Sue, Ruth, Rachel, Aevon, and his no-name friend with the Nanaimo bars.

The originals: my brothers and sisters, my parents—the late Jim and Gwen Kimmett.

The beautiful kids: Brendan and Laurel.

AUTHOR
BIO

Deborah Kimmett is a trailblazer in Canadian comedy. Having performed on Canadian stage and screen across North America, she's a regular on CBC Radio (*The Debaters* and *Laugh Out Loud*). She is the author of three books: *Reality Is Overrated*, *Outrunning Crazy*, and *That Which Doesn't Kill You Makes You Funnier*. She was twice nominated for a National Magazine Award for Humour, and her play *Miracle Mother* was shortlisted for the Governor General's Literary Award for Drama. Kimmett lives in Toronto.